THE MARIAN CATECHISM

THE MARIAN CATECHISM

FR. ROBERT J. FOX

OUR SUNDAY VISITOR, INC.
Noll Plaza
Huntington, Indiana 46750

Nihil Obstat:
Rev. Adam D. Schmitt
Censor Librorum

Imprimatur:
✠Leo A. Pursley, D.D.
Bishop of Fort Wayne-South Bend
January 2, 1976

The Nihil Obstat and Imprimatur are official declarations
that a book or pamphlet is free of doctrinal or moral
error. No implication is contained therein that those who
have granted the Nihil Obstat or Imprimatur agree with the
contents, opinions or statements expressed.

ISBN: 0-87973-766-2
Library of Congress Catalog Card Number: 75-45756

First Printing, Mar. 1976
Second Printing, Nov. 1976

Cover Design by Eric Nesheim

Published, printed and bound in the
U.S.A. by
Our Sunday Visitor, Inc.
Noll Plaza
Huntington, Indiana   46750

766

TABLE OF CONTENTS

INTRODUCTION

This catechism on Mary was written out of love for the Mother of God. At the same time it was written out of love for the entire Blessed Trinity and the Catholic Church which is Christ's Mystical Body. Mary must be understood and loved in relationship to Jesus Christ, the entire Trinity and the Church. True devotion to Mary must never be separated from the fullness of true faith.

To have a fullness of true faith, to understand the Church as Christ intended, both in God's relationship to man and man's relationship to God, one must appreciate Mary's role in salvation. Jesus Christ, the invisible Head of the Church, was "born of a woman." The opening pages of the Bible tell us of the fall and the promised Redeemer and of the woman whose child would crush the head of the devil. She would be an enemy of the forces of evil which would struggle for the souls of men.

When one knows and loves Mary better, that person knows and loves Jesus better. Also, one knows and loves the Church better. The person is then able to love and better serve God the Father, God the Son and God the Holy Spirit.

Mary has not been known, loved and emphasized too much, thus distracting from Jesus Christ. Mary has been known and loved and emphasized too little, not only by Christians other than Catholics, but by Catholics themselves. Because the role of Mary, according to God's plan in salvation, is too little known, Jesus and the Church are not known and loved as they should be. For too long, Christians have ignored the Mother of the Church, the Woman of Faith, that perfect Christian. Therefore, their identity with Jesus in the Church has been harmed.

Sometimes Catholics devoted to the Rosary and the Brown Scapular of Our Lady of Mt. Carmel may come on strong, desiring others to live such practices. Perhaps they themselves, sometimes, do not properly understand these devotions in relation to Jesus Christ, the Church and even Mary herself. Then, too, others may stress approved revelations such as Fatima, Lourdes or those of earlier times and place them on the same level as Sacred Scripture and the defined doctrines of the Church. I do not question their sincerity nor, certainly, their zeal. But such practices, "recommended by the teaching authority of the Church in the course of centuries" must also be understood in relationship to the total teachings of the Church and its chief book, the Holy Bible.

It is the purpose of this catechism on Mary, then, to bring its readers and those who study and meditate on it to a greater knowledge and love of Mary, the Mother of the Church. Seen as Daughter of God the Father, Spouse of the Holy Spirit and Mother of the Son, one will not consider this holy creature as competing with her Son, Jesus. Then the time-tested devotions will be understood within the total context of divine revelation. Consequently, the Rosary, the Scapular, etc., will not need to be, and should not be, "forced" upon anyone. They will have such an inner attractiveness, coming as they do from the heart of Christ Himself, Who has loving compassion on all men, that God's people of all ages will experience a deep desire to love God's Mother in a way revealed, ultimately, by heaven itself.

For what age is this catechism on Mary intended? It is intended for youngsters of all ages. There is no age limit. Adults, who are invited also to use it, are asked to remember, "Unless you be converted and become as little children . . ."

In writing and answering questions about Mary, one is doing the same for Christ, the Church and the Blessed Trinity Who has done great things for her. Because God has done great things for Mary, He has done great and holy things for us in giving us Mary in order to give us Jesus Who in turn gives us the Church. The invisible Head of the Church is the Son of Mary.

This catechism on Mary does not say all there is to say about God's Mother. That would be impossible. I am reminded here of the Apostle of Love, St. John, who wrote at the end of his Gospel, "If all were written down, the world itself, I suppose, would not hold all the books that would have to be written." If the world cannot hold all that would have to be written about Jesus, the Son, neither can it contain the story of Mary, who reflects His beauty and receives all from Him.

FATHER ROBERT J. FOX

HOW TO USE THIS CATECHISM ON MARY

Adults should find no difficulty in studying or discussing this catechism among themselves. The use of this catechism for children and young people, however, will require parental and teacher guidance. The author suggests the methods below.

• Younger children should study only the second or *italicized* answer. Each question is answered twice. The first answer is for older students and adults. The second, more simple and concise, is for children of early years in school.

• Older students and adults may find the concise italicized answer a summary of the more in-depth answer.

• Very young children will need help in studying at home, as in class. This will give parents an opportunity to share their faith with their children as the primary educators and formers in the faith, a God-given privilege and duty. As the questions and answers develop further on in the catechism, they will need rephrasing and simplification for younger children.

• The author is not against memorizing certain basic Catholic teachings. The nature of this catechism, for the most part, however, does not lend itself to that. It should be acceptable if the young person can give the answer substantially, showing a basic comprehension. Being able to answer correctly, but using one's own words, will show that knowledge of the answer is from love for the persons of Jesus and

Mary. This will be the case where parent or teacher (group leader) has a deep faith and love which will thus be communicated.

• The parent or teacher (group leader) should be willing to expand or simplify the questions and answers according to individual needs of the student or class. The answers should not be interpreted as a rigid border within which one must stay. It is only necessary that one remain true to the Catholic faith, whatever words and examples are used to communicate the fullness of the one true faith.

• The catechism need not be covered all in one year, especially for younger children in the first few years of school. It may be better to keep the more advanced questions and answers for another year. The truths of faith should not be relearned, nor what is taught once be untaught. This catechism is designed to serve the concentric method of gradually advancing in greater depth the fullness of true faith.

• By having young people go through this catechism more than once, the depth of appreciation of God's Mother and her role in the economy of salvation may well be served. Going through, from beginning to end, especially in different years, students will understand concentrically, in greater depth, Mary's role relating to Jesus Christ.

• At the end of each chapter is a summary of truths given in the answers to the questions. When used as class or group discussion, the summary could be read, even explained, according to individual or class needs, so as to prepare the group for home study. They will then give some stimulation for individual study. Before passing on to another lesson, the summary could be read again by everyone as a group, bringing to mind the lesson and truths of faith just covered. It is always well to prepare for home study so that the student does not meet subjects for the first time completely unacquainted.

• Questions to be answered are found at the end of each chapter on a work page. The answers can be written out for homework. To answer them correctly, comprehension of the total chapter is required. Answering the questions correctly will give evidence of each student's prayerful thinking and of the student's having studied the lessons. Special help will be needed at home by very young students. Again, this will bring parents into child-formation in faith.

• Teachers should feel free to develop questions other than those given in the chapter for homework.

• Students should learn to strive to implement the truths of their faith into their daily spiritual lives. Suggested practices are given on each work page. Individuals or groups may decide upon other practices so as to live their faith in union with Jesus and Mary.

1

CREATION OF MARY
(Questions 1-10)

1. WHO IS MARY?

Mary is the Mother of our Lord Jesus Christ. Mary is our Mother by grace.

(Mary is the Mother of our Lord.)

2. WHO IS JESUS CHRIST?

Jesus Christ is our Lord, God and Savior. Jesus is both God and man. Jesus is the true Son of God and the true Son of Mary.

(Jesus Christ is our Lord and Savior.)

3. DOES THIS MEAN THAT MARY IS THE MOTHER OF GOD?

Yes. Mary is the true Mother of God. Her Son Jesus Christ is the Second Person of the Blessed Trinity.

(Yes. Mary is the true Mother of God.)

4. WHO IS THE FATHER OF JESUS CHRIST?

God the Father, the First Person of the Blessed Trinity, is the true and real Father of Jesus Christ.

(God the Father.)

5. WHO IS ST. JOSEPH?

St. Joseph is the real husband of Mary. St. Joseph is the foster father of Jesus Christ. He was the protector of the Holy Family. St. Joseph represented God the Father on earth to Jesus Christ. He was a very holy and just man. Today Joseph ranks in honor in heaven after Jesus and Mary.

(St. Joseph is the husband of Mary and foster father of Jesus.)

6. WHAT RELATIONSHIP DID MARY HAVE TO THE HOLY SPIRIT?

Mary conceived the Child Jesus through the Holy Spirit. Even though St. Joseph was the true husband of Mary, it was by the Holy Spirit that Mary became the Mother of Jesus.

(By the power of the Holy Spirit Mary became the Mother of Jesus.)

7. WHAT RELATIONSHIP DOES MARY HAVE TO THE BLESSED TRINITY?

Mary is the first Daughter of God the Father. Mary is the Mother of God the Son. Mary is the Spouse of the Holy Spirit.

(Mary is closer to all Three Persons in God than anyone else.)

8. WAS MARY THE DAUGHTER OF ADAM?

Yes. Mary descended from Adam like everyone else in the human race. Our first parents were Adam and Eve. Jesus is like a new Adam. Mary is like a new

Eve. Mary's parents were St. Anne and St. Joachim.

(Yes, Mary came from the first man and woman like everyone else.)

9. HOW IS JESUS LIKE A NEW ADAM?

Adam was the first man. By his sin the whole human race fell. We all inherit original sin from Adam. We are born with sin on our souls. Jesus redeemed us from sin by dying on the cross for us. Adam lost grace for us. Jesus merited grace for us.

(The first Adam lost grace for us. Jesus won grace back for us.)

10. HOW IS MARY LIKE A NEW EVE?

Even while on earth Mary was holy, innocent, most pure and immaculate. She was in grace when God made her, just as God made Adam and Eve in grace. The first Eve cooperated with Adam in sinning. Mary cooperated with Jesus to bring us back to grace.

(The first Eve helped Adam sin. Mary helped Jesus win us grace.)

SUMMARY:

Mary is the Mother of God. Yet Mary was created in time. God made the soul of Mary out of nothing. All people, including Mary, descended from Adam and Eve whom God first made from the dust of the earth and breathed living souls into them. When God made the souls of Adam and Eve He made their souls in grace. They lost that grace. When

God made the soul of Mary, He made her soul in grace, too; but Mary never lost grace.

After Jesus, Mary is nearest to God of all the things that God has created.

QUESTIONS:

    1. Did Mary and Joseph get married?
    2. Who took the place of Adam and Eve?
    3. How were Eve and Mary alike?
    4. How were Eve and Mary not alike?
    5. What relationship does Mary have to each Person of the Blessed Trinity?

PRACTICE:

Think of all Three Persons of the Blessed Trinity to Whom Mary has a special relation. Then thank God for creating Mary to be such a wonderful creature.

2

MARY, CREATED WITHOUT SIN
(Questions 11-18)

11. WHAT IS THAT PRIVILEGE OF MARY CALLED WHEREBY SHE WAS MADE WITHOUT SIN?

It is called the Immaculate Conception. At the first instant that God made the soul of Mary He kept her free from all stain of original sin. Sin never touched her soul in the slightest degree.

(It is called the Immaculate Conception, because Mary was always without sin.)

12. WHEN DID THE CATHOLIC CHURCH PRO-CLAIM THE IMMACULATE CONCEPTION TO BE A DOCTRINE OF CATHOLIC FAITH?

Pope Pius IX proclaimed the Immaculate Conception on December 8; 1854. The Pope stated that the truth that Mary "was preserved free from all stain of original sin, has been revealed by God, and therefore is to be firmly and constantly believed by all the faithful."

(The Catholic Church said over a hundred years ago that we must believe in the Immaculate Conception.)

13. DID THE BLESSED VIRGIN GIVE THE WORLD

A SIGN TO APPROVE THE CHURCH'S PROCLAIMING HER IMMACULATE CONCEPTION?

Yes. According to Pope Pius XII, when in 1954 he called for a Marian Year to celebrate the 100th anniversary of the definition of the Immaculate Conception, Mary did give a sign. The Pope wrote:

"Four years had not yet elapsed when, in the French town at the foot of the Pyrenees, the Virgin Mother showed herself to a simple and innocent girl at the grotto of Massabielle and to this same girl, earnestly inquiring the name of her with whose vision she was favored, with eyes raised to heaven and sweetly smiling, she replied, 'I am the Immaculate Conception.' " When the world learned of the visions, thousands of people from every country came to Lourdes where Mary appeared to St. Bernadette and where "miraculous favors were granted them, which excited the admiration of all and confirmed the Catholic religion as the only one given approval by God." (Cf. *Fulgens Corona.*)

(Mary appeared to St. Bernadette in Lourdes, France, and said, "I am the Immaculate Conception.")

14. WAS ANYONE ELSE EVER MADE WITHOUT ORIGINAL SIN?

Yes. Jesus Christ was created free from original sin. That is because Jesus was God and could have no sin.

(Yes. Jesus, because He was God and could have no sin on His soul.)

15. IF MARY WAS CREATED WITHOUT ORIGI-

NAL SIN DID SHE EVER COMMIT ANY SINS HERSELF?

No. Mary never committed the slightest sin. God made her full of grace. Mary never committed even the smallest sin because she was very holy.

(Mary never committed any sins.)

16. IF MARY WAS ALWAYS WITHOUT SIN, DID SHE NEED TO BE REDEEMED?

Yes. Jesus Christ her Son redeemed her, too. Jesus redeemed us all by His life, death and resurrection. Jesus redeemed His Mother so perfectly that at the very moment God made her soul He put sanctifying grace into it.

(Yes. Jesus died on the cross for Mary, too.)

17. HOW COULD JESUS REDEEM MARY'S SOUL WHEN JESUS HAD NOT YET BEEN BORN OR DIED ON THE CROSS WHEN GOD MADE MARY?

Jesus redeemed Mary's soul by anticipation. God is not restricted by our time. All that Jesus would do in His life upon earth was always in the mind of God. Mary was always there, too. Mary knew when her Son was suffering so much that He was suffering for her, too. Jesus merited for Mary all her privileges and all her graces.

(God kept Mary from sin when He made her for He knew Jesus would die for her later.)

18. WAS MARY SOMETIMES MOVED TO SIN?

No. Because of Adam's sin we inherit weakness.

We are inclined to sense pleasures which are against right reason and the Ten Commandments. But Mary was full of grace and free of these consequences of original sin.

(No. Mary never wanted to sin.)

SUMMARY:

God always knew He would one day create a woman to become His Mother. That woman was Mary. When God made her, He made her so holy that never for an instant was the sweet soul of Mary touched by original sin. God made Mary without sin and Mary never committed any personal sins during her whole life.

Still, it was Jesus Who redeemed Mary. At the moment God made the soul of His Mother, God kept from happening what should have happened otherwise. As a descendant of Adam, Mary also should have inherited original sin. She did not. God looked ahead to the life, death and resurrection of Jesus. The saving graces of Jesus came to Mary ahead of time. God created Mary without sin. Later Jesus would die on the cross to earn that privilege for His Mother.

QUESTIONS:

1. What is meant by the Immaculate Conception?

2. Why could Jesus have no sin on His soul when God created a soul for Jesus?

3. Did Mary know that Jesus was suffering for her, too, on the cross?

PRACTICE:

Wear the Miraculous Medal to remind you that Mary was conceived without original sin, that she never committed the slightest sin. It will help you remember that as Mary's child you should not sin, but pray when you are tempted.

3

MARY, EVER-VIRGIN
(Questions 19-26)

19. WHEN IS MARY FIRST MENTIONED IN THE BIBLE?

In Genesis, the first book of the Bible. Many scholars believe that when God cursed the serpent, He was speaking of the enmity between man and the devil, and that the woman referred to is Mary and her offspring, Jesus. Through Jesus the head of the serpent would be crushed.

(Scholars believe that Mary is first mentioned in the Bible on its first pages.)

20. DID MARY AND JOSEPH HAVE OTHER CHILDREN BESIDES JESUS?

No. Jesus was the only child born of Mary.

(No. Jesus had no brothers or sisters.)

21. WHAT DOES THE BIBLE MEAN WHEN IT SPEAKS OF BROTHERS AND SISTERS OF JESUS?

The Bible is speaking about relatives of our Lord. Jesus had no brothers and sisters from Mary and Joseph. The Bible speaks of relatives as "brethren," meaning "brothers and sisters."

(In the Bible the cousins of Jesus are called His brothers and sisters.)

22. WAS MARY ALWAYS A VIRGIN?

Yes. After the birth of Jesus, Mary continued always to be a virgin, just as she had been before marrying Joseph. Mary and Joseph offered their bodies and souls entirely to the love of God in perfect virginity.

(Mary was always the Blessed Virgin.)

23. DID MARY AND JOSEPH BOTH TAKE THE VOW OF VIRGINITY?

Yes. Their love for each other in God was so perfect that even though they were husband and wife they had agreed always to be virgins. We know this from the way Mary talked to the Angel Gabriel when it was announced that Mary was to become the Mother of the Messiah.

(Mary and Joseph both promised God always to be virgins.)

24. WHAT DID MARY ASK THE ANGEL GABRIEL ABOUT HER VIRGINITY?

Mary said to the angel, "But how can this come about, since I am a virgin?" "The Holy Spirit will come upon you," the angel answered, "and the power of the Most High will cover you with its shadow. And so the child will be holy and will be called Son of God" (Luke 1:34-35).

(Mary asked the angel if God wanted her to remain a virgin. The angel said, "Yes.")

25. WHAT DO WE KNOW FROM THE BIBLE RE-

GARDING ST. JOSEPH THAT HE WAS NOT THE NATURAL FATHER OF JESUS?

St. Matthew's Gospel says that Mary was betrothed to Joseph "but before they came to live together she was found to be with child through the Holy Spirit." Now Joseph did not know it was through the power of the Holy Spirit and so he was very much concerned, being a just man. The angel of the Lord appeared to him in a dream and said, "Joseph, son of David, do not be afraid to take Mary home as your wife, because she has conceived what is in her by the Holy Spirit. She will give birth to a son and you must name him Jesus, because he is the one who is to save his people from their sins."

(St. Joseph was surprised that Mary was with child. God told St. Joseph that the Holy Spirit gave Mary the child.)

26. DID THE OLD TESTAMENT OF THE BIBLE SAY ANYTHING ABOUT THE MOTHER OF THE SAVIOR BEING A VIRGIN?

Yes. Right after the above words, St. Matthew quotes the Old-Testament words of Isaiah the Prophet: "Now all this took place to fulfill the words spoken by the Lord through the prophet: 'The virgin will conceive and give birth to a son and they will call him Emmanuel, which means "God-is-with-us." ' "

(Yes. Even before Mary was born the Bible said a virgin would have a child.)

SUMMARY:

Mary truly became the Mother of Jesus and the

Mother of God. Still, Mary did not become a mother like other women. Mary and Joseph did not express their love for each other entirely like other husbands and wives. Mary and Joseph offered themselves, body and soul, entirely to God. Joseph was not needed for Mary to become a mother. It was the Holy Spirit that came down on Mary like a shadow. The Holy Spirit penetrated Mary like the sun shining through crystal. Jesus, then, had no human father. Joseph took the place of a father. We call Joseph, then, the foster father of Jesus. Mary, however, was the true Mother of Jesus. After the Holy Spirit overshadowed Mary, she carried the Infant Jesus in her womb until He was born on the first Christmas.

QUESTIONS:

1. What is the first thing the Bible says about Mary?

2. Can we tell from the Bible that Joseph knew he was not the father of Mary's child?

3. How many children did Mary and Joseph have?

4. What did Mary and the Angel Gabriel talk about?

PRACTICE:

Think how completely holy and pure God's Mother always was. Ask Mary to keep you always holy in all your thoughts, words and actions.

4

MOTHER OF THE MESSIAH
AND MOTHER OF MEN
(Questions 27-36)

27. WHAT ARE THE FIRST WORDS IN THE BIBLE WHERE GOD PROMISES A SAVIOR?

The words are found in Genesis, chapter 3, verse 15, the first book of the Bible. There it says: "I will put enmity between you and the woman, and between your offspring and hers. He will strike at your head, while you strike at his heel."

(In the first pages of the Bible it says the woman would crush the head of the serpent by the child she would have.)

28. WHEN WERE THESE WORDS FROM GENESIS FIRST UNDERSTOOD TO MEAN JESUS AND HIS MOTHER?

Very early in Christian history. Spiritual writers as early as the second century see the woman to be Mary and the offspring to be Jesus, the Messiah. The early writers pointed out that the disbelief and disobedience of Eve brought ruin to mankind. The faith and obedience of Mary brought salvation.

(The first Christians knew they meant Mary would be an enemy of the devil by giving us Jesus.)

29. WHAT IS MEANT BY MESSIAH?

Messiah means "anointed one." That, too, is the meaning of the word "Christ." The word "Christ" or "anointed one" became added to "Jesus." The Messiah was the one the prophets pointed to as a future king who would protect God's people. He would come from the family or house of David.

(Messiah is a name for Jesus Christ.)

30. DOES THIS MEAN THAT GENESIS, CHAPTER 3, VERSE 15, IS MESSIANIC-MARIAN?

Yes. Those first words in the Bible promising the world a Savior refer to both Jesus and Mary. From the very beginning of the history of true religion, Jesus and Mary are placed together. Mary and Jesus are inseparable.

(Yes. The first pages of the Bible direct us to both Jesus and Mary.)

31. WHEN DID THE CHURCH FIRST BELIEVE IN THE IMMACULATE CONCEPTION?

Very early. The Council of Ephesus called Mary, "Mother of God." Certainly, the Mother of God could never have been touched by sin.

(The Catholic Church has always believed in the Immaculate Conception.)

32. WHEN DID CHRISTIANS FIRST BEGIN TO CELEBRATE THE FEAST OF THE IMMACULATE CONCEPTION?

A feast of the Immaculate Conception was celebrated each year in the Eastern part of the world in the last half of the seventh century. Pope Sixtus IV approved a special liturgy for the Immaculate Conception in 1476. In 1568 Pope St. Pius VI made the Feast of the Immaculate Conception a holy day of obligation to be celebrated by Catholics all over the world. In 1846 the Immaculate Conception was made patroness of the United States.

(Over 1,300 years ago Christians had a feast in honor of the Immaculate Conception.)

33. WHAT IS MEANT BY A HOLY DAY OF OBLIGATION?

A holy day of obligation is a day when Catholics are obligated in conscience, if physically possible, to worship God through participation in the holy sacrifice of the Mass, the same as on the fifty-two Sundays of the year.

(A holy day of obligation means Catholics must take part in the sacrifice of the Mass, same as on Sundays.)

34. AT WHAT AGE DOES THE OBLIGATION TO PARTICIPATE AT MASS ON SUNDAYS AND OTHER HOLY DAYS OF OBLIGATION BEGIN?

All baptized persons in the Catholic Church who have attained the use of reason and are seven years of age must participate at Mass on these days.

(The obligation to worship God on Sundays and all other holy days of obligation begins when one has reached the use of reason and is seven years of age.)

35. CAN WE SPEAK OF MARY AS HAVING BEEN CLEANSED FROM ORIGINAL SIN?

No. There was never any sin on her soul to be cleansed.

(No. Mary did not have to be washed from sin she never had.)

36. WHAT IS MEANT BY THE SOULS OF JESUS AND MARY?

Mary and Jesus each had a created soul, just as we do. As God, Jesus had no beginning. He always was and always will be. But in time, the Blessed Trinity created a human soul for Jesus as well as a human body. Mary did not exist before God created her soul. The soul is a spirit made in the image and likeness of God and it will never die.

(Jesus and Mary had souls that were spirits which could never die.)

SUMMARY:

Mary became not only the Mother of Jesus, the Messiah, but also the Mother of all men. Jesus was the Messiah, the one God's chosen people waited for a long time to save them from their sins. When the Messiah finally came, He came through Mary. Already in the Old Testament of the Bible, when God's Word speaks about a Messiah who was coming, the Bible also spoke about the woman through whom the Savior would come.

Mary and Jesus are always inseparable. By giving the world its Messiah, Mary also became the Mother of all men who would receive grace from

Jesus. The Catholic Church teaches us the importance of Mary by making some of her feasts, like the Assumption on August 15 and the Immaculate Conception on December 8, holy days of obligation for Catholics.

QUESTIONS:

1. Who spoke the very first words about Mary?
2. How soon after the fall of Adam and Eve did God promise a Savior?
3. Was Mary mentioned in some way when God promised a Savior?
4. Why can we not speak of Mary as being cleansed from original sin?

PRACTICE:

Think of how God always speaks of Mary together with Jesus. Let us always remember to think of Jesus when we pray to Mary.

5

MARY, FULL OF GRACE
(Questions 37-49)

37. DOES THE BIBLE SAY THAT MARY IS GREAT?

Yes. The Bible is the recorded Word of God. It was written under the inspiration of the Holy Spirit. The Holy Spirit is the Spouse of the Virgin Mary. The Bible therefore tells us much about Mary's greatness.

(From the Bible we know that Mary is greater than all angels and saints.)

38. WHERE IN THE BIBLE DOES IT TELL OF MARY'S GREATNESS?

The greatness of Mary comes from her being most blessed. But Mary does not claim that her great grace comes from herself. Mary was most humble. In the first chapter of St. Luke's Gospel we hear the Angel Gabriel address Mary as "full of grace." Heaven calls her the highly favored one. It was under the power of the Holy Spirit that Mary prayed the prayer called "The Magnificat." In that prayer Mary says, "My soul proclaims the greatness of the Lord." Whenever Mary is mentioned in the Old or New Testament she is seen as most highly favored by God, next to the Savior.

(From beginning to end, the Bible tells us of Mary's greatness.)

39. DID ANYONE ELSE BESIDES THE ANGEL GABRIEL SPEAK OF MARY'S GREATNESS THROUGH THE POWER OF THE HOLY SPIRIT?

Yes. Elizabeth, the cousin of Mary and who was the mother of John the Baptist, was in her sixth month with child when Mary came to visit her. As soon as Mary greeted Elizabeth, the Bible says, "Elizabeth was filled with the Holy Spirit. She gave a loud cry and said, 'Of all women you are the most blessed, and blessed is the fruit of your womb. Why should I be honored with a visit from the mother of my Lord?' " (Luke 1:41-44).

(God Himself, through the angel and Mary's cousin Elizabeth, tells us how great Mary is.)

40. DID THE ANGEL GABRIEL SAY THAT THE HOLY SPIRIT WOULD BE PART OF MARY'S BECOMING GOD'S MOTHER?

Yes. The Angel Gabriel who was sent by God to a town in Galilee called Nazareth, to a virgin (whose name was Mary) betrothed to a man named Joseph, of the House of David, spoke this way: "The Holy Spirit will come upon you and the power of the Most High will cover you with its shadow. And so the child will be holy and will be called Son of God" (Luke 1:26-36).

(Yes. The Angel Gabriel said that Mary would become the Mother of God by the power of the Holy Spirit.)

41. WHY DID GOD KEEP MARY FREE FROM ORIGINAL SIN AND ALL PERSONAL SINS?

God kept Mary free from original sin and all sin because He loved her more than all other created persons and wanted her to be Jesus' Mother. She was to crush the head of the serpent, the devil, by the fruit of her womb. Therefore, Mary herself was never to be under any power of the devil.

(God kept Mary free from all sin to make her worthy to be Jesus' Mother.)

42. WHY DID GOD MAKE MARY FULL OF GRACE?

God made Mary "full of grace" because she was chosen to become the Mother of the author and source of grace. God always knew and loved Mary from all eternity. Even though God did not create her until about 2,000 years ago, God always knew and loved her in His mind. When He made her, God made Mary beautiful and full of grace so that she would be worthy to be the Mother of His Son.

(God made Mary full of grace because she was to be the Mother of Jesus Who is the author of grace.)

43. WAS MARY THEN WORTHY TO BE THE MOTHER OF GOD?

Not by her own power. Mary was made like the rest of us, except that she was made full of grace. Mary was always loved by God more than all other angels and saints, or people taken together. Jesus Christ, her Son, merited for His Mother, her greatness. Mary never considered herself worthy. It was God Who made her worthy.

(Yes. Mary was worthy to be the Mother of God because God made her worthy.)

44. DID JESUS EVER PUBLICLY PRAISE HIS MOTHER?

Yes. St. Luke tells us that when a woman praised Mary, Jesus agreed, saying: "Yes, indeed, blessed are they who hear the word of God and follow it."

(Yes.)

45. WHAT DOES MERIT MEAN?

Merit means the right to a reward promised by God for good and supernatural work done for God. Jesus Christ, our Savior, true God and true man, merited the salvation of all peoples for all time. The merits of Jesus are infinite, without limit.

(To merit means to have a right to something because of a promise.)

46. CAN WE REJECT THE MERITS OF JESUS CHRIST?

Yes, because each one of us has a free will. God does not force the merits of His Son Jesus upon us. When we sin by disobeying the Ten Commandments of God and the laws of the Church we reject the merits of Jesus Christ. When we live our faith in hope and love and do good works for the love of God, and love our neighbor for the love of God, then we draw from the merits of Jesus Christ.

(Yes. Jesus does not force us to accept His good gifts. We can turn away from Jesus.)

47. DID ANYONE EVER MERIT MORE THAN HE NEEDED?

Yes, great saints did. The ever-virgin Mother of God, above all, merited a superabundance of merits through her Son Jesus Christ.

(Yes. Mary, God's Mother, especially merited from Jesus more than she needed for herself.)

48. DID ANYONE EVER CO-MERIT WITH CHRIST?

Yes; but remember the merits of salvation were first earned by our Lord Jesus Christ. St. Paul in the Bible teaches that we can win salvation only by the grace first merited by Jesus Christ. St. Peter, the first Pope, said, "Neither is there salvation in any other" than Jesus Christ our Lord. To co-merit means that one lives a Christian life of love and faith so perfectly that he draws from the merits of Jesus, not only for himself, but for others.

(Yes. Mary cooperated with Jesus perfectly.)

49. WHO MORE THAN ANY OTHER CREATURE CO-MERITED WITH CHRIST?

Mary, the Mother of Jesus, co-merited with her Son. Mary was more powerful than any other in co-operating with Jesus and was under Him as a creature is under its Maker.

(Mary cooperated with Jesus and merited with Him more than all others.)

SUMMARY:

What a beautiful name heaven gives Mary. The

Angel Gabriel does not call her "Mary." Rather, the title by which the angel hails her is "full of grace." Mary was truly full of grace, created in grace from the first moment God made her soul. Then, too, Mary always cooperated perfectly in faith with grace under the action of the Holy Spirit. Mary was not worthy of her own power to be God's Mother. Mary was made worthy by God creating her full of grace. Mary's very name, "full of grace," tells us that Mary was never touched by any sin.

Jesus merited grace for His Mother and the whole world. Great saints, especially God's Mother, cooperated so perfectly with God's grace that they merited from Jesus grace for other members of the human family.

QUESTIONS:

1. Did Mary merit being full of grace?
2. What name did the Angel Gabriel give Mary? Why?
3. To whom did Mary give the credit for her being so great?
4. What does co-merit mean?
5. Was Mary only greater than any one angel or saint, or greater than all of them together?

PRACTICE:

Honor Mary more than all angels and saints. Tell Mary often that you love and honor her for her greatness. Give the credit for Mary's being full of grace to God. Then imitate Mary herself by having deep faith and accepting the graces God gives.

6

MARY DEPENDS ON JESUS
(Questions 50-59)

50. WHAT MADE MARY SO POWERFUL AS TO INFLUENCE THE SAVING OF SOULS?

The Blessed Virgin's power to influence the salvation of men did not come from any inner necessity of God but completely from the good pleasure of God. Mary is the "Mother of divine grace" and "Virgin most powerful" because God willed that, under Christ, Mary should be above all others, most powerful with the Blessed Trinity.

(God Himself made Mary powerful so that she could work with Jesus in saving souls.)

51. GOD DID NOT HAVE TO MAKE MARY SO POWERFUL, AS CO-MERITER, YET, WHAT DID GOD DO THAT MADE HER SO GREAT?

God made the Blessed Virgin, after Jesus, the highest one in sanctity. God made Mary "full of grace." Mary is more pleasing to God than all lesser creatures.

(God made Mary Jesus' Mother; but first God made her "full of grace" and without sin of any kind.)

52. IS MARY GREATER THAN THE ANGELS?

Yes, Mary is greater than all the nine choirs of

angels in heaven. Mary is the Queen of angels and saints.

(Yes. Mary is loved by God and is greater than all other creatures of God.)

53. HOW CAN MARY BE GREATER THAN THE ANGELS WHEN ANGELS ARE SUPERIOR TO MAN?

The Bible says that God made man a little less than the angels. Angels are created spirits without bodies, having understanding and free will. It is the grace of Mary and her dignity as the Mother of God that places her above not only some but all of the angels. God loved Mary more than all men and all angels. Therefore, God gave Mary's soul more grace than all angels and men.

(It is the great grace in Mary's soul that makes her greater than the angels.)

54. CAN MARY EVER BE SEPARATED FROM JESUS CHRIST?

No. In the Virgin Mary everything is related to Jesus Christ. Everything great and holy about Mary depends totally on Jesus.

(No. Mary and Jesus are perfectly one in love.)

55. WHOM DID THE BLESSED TRINITY DECIDE TO PLACE ON EARTH FIRST, GOD THE SON AS MAN OR MARY HIS MOTHER?

Neither. It was with one single thought that God was determined to make Mary and that God the Son should become man through Mary to save the world.

Mary and Jesus are inseparable. They have always been united in God's mind.

(God decided at one and the same moment to make Jesus and Mary. God always knew He would do this.)

56. WHEN DID GOD FIRST DECIDE TO MAKE ADAM AND EVE, JESUS AND MARY?

God always knew He would make Adam and Eve, and that the Son of God would become man in Jesus Christ through Mary. The Person of Jesus was not made, but always was and always will be. God made a body for God the Son from the body of Mary. God always knew that the first two people would sin. However, God would draw good from the evil of the fall by giving us Jesus through Mary.

(God knows everything at all times. He always knew He would make them.)

57. WAS MARY FREE TO BECOME THE MOTHER OF JESUS, OR DID SHE HAVE TO?

Mary freely accepted the will of God to become the Mother of the Messiah. When she fully understood the will of God, that she was to remain a virgin, that the Holy Spirit was to overshadow her, Mary then answered, "I am the handmaid of the Lord; let what you have said be done to me" (Luke 1:38). Mary was perfectly free in saying "yes" to God.

(God asked Mary if she would become the Mother of God. Mary said, "Yes.")

58. WHAT DOES THE CHURCH MEAN BY THE REDEMPTION?

The redemption refers to the life of sacrifice which Jesus lived upon earth to win back for mankind friendship with God. Jesus became our Redeemer by meriting our salvation through His life and death on the cross. Mankind lost grace by the sin of Adam. The devil then had a certain claim over Adam and his descendants. Jesus redeemed us. The price of our redemption was the shedding of His precious blood. Jesus' redemption means He has reclaimed us for heaven.

(Redemption means to redeem or buy back. Jesus shed His blood to redeem our souls for heaven.)

59. WHAT IS MEANT BY ATONEMENT?

Atonement means the same as reparation, or making good for any wrong or injury done to another. By sin man was separated from God. God took mankind's sin upon Himself in Jesus Christ and made up for our sins. Jesus atoned, that is, He made it possible for men to be one with God through grace again.

(Atonement means to become one with another. Jesus died on the cross to make us one with His heavenly Father.)

SUMMARY:

Catholic understanding and devotion to Mary is understood only by remembering that Mary depends upon Jesus for everything. Mary herself understood that. Mary said, "He Who is mighty has done great things for me." Mary was perfectly humble. God Himself wanted to use Mary as His instrument in giving glory to the Blessed Trinity and in bringing salvation to men. All of Mary's greatness depends upon her being the Mother of Jesus Who is the Son of God.

Mary was not forced by God to be His Mother. Mary willed to do whatever God wanted. Mary brought Jesus into our world so He could redeem us from our sins. Jesus made perfect atonement, that is, Jesus made up to God the Father for the sins of the world, by the shedding of His precious blood on the cross.

QUESTIONS:

1. Where does Mary get her power to help in the saving of souls?

2. Why did God give Mary more grace than all the angels and all men?

3. When did God decide to create Mary?

4. What did Mary give the world?

5. How did Jesus redeem the world?

PRACTICE:

Always keep in mind that without Jesus you can do nothing. In Jesus we live, move and have our being. Take Mary as your model in depending on Jesus for everything.

7

MARY COOPERATES WITH JESUS
(Questions 60-69)

60. DID JESUS CHRIST REALLY BECOME OUR BROTHER?

Yes. All who are baptized into Jesus Christ become His brothers and sisters. The indelible seal of Jesus is stamped upon the soul forever. Baptism gives us grace for the first time, making us live in Jesus Christ. Jesus becomes our brother but is still our Lord.

(Yes. Jesus really became one of our human race. By grace Jesus puts His own life into our souls.)

61. WHAT IS THE SANCTIFYING GRACE WHICH BAPTISM GIVES US FOR THE FIRST TIME?

Sanctifying grace is a sharing in the very life of God. Jesus said: "I am Life. . . . I have come that you may have life and have it more abundantly. . . . Unless you eat the flesh of the Son of Man and drink His blood you shall not have life in you. . . . I am the Vine, you are the branches; He who abides in me and I in him, the same bears much fruit." By sanctifying grace Jesus lives in us and we live in Jesus. We become one in Jesus in His Church which is His Mystical Body.

(Grace is the sharing by our soul in the very God-life of Jesus.)

62. DID MARY COOPERATE WITH JESUS IN MAKING ATONEMENT?

Yes. Mary shared in the role of Jesus in bringing peace (reconciliation) between His heavenly Father and mankind.

(Yes. Mary more than anyone else helped Jesus make people one with God the Father.)

63. WHAT DID VATICAN COUNCIL II SAY ABOUT MARY SUPPORTING JESUS' ACTS OF REDEMPTION?

Vatican II said the following about Mary and Jesus: "The Blessed Virgin advanced in her pilgrimage of faith, and faithfully persevered in her union with her Son unto the cross, where she stood, in keeping with the divine plan, grieving exceedingly with her only-begotten Son, uniting herself with a maternal heart with his sacrifice, and lovingly consenting to the immolation of this victim, which she herself had brought forth."

(The Pope and bishops of the world said that Mary by faith and love did the same things in her heart that Jesus did in His sufferings so as to save the world.)

64. DID MARY HAVE FAITH WHEN SHE WAS ON EARTH?

Yes. The Bible informs us that Mary was the great Woman of Faith. Mary's great faith made her especially blessed. She had to believe in God and believe her Son Jesus was God Himself. Mary's faith

45

was so perfect that she is the perfect model of the Church and of the perfect Christian.

(Yes. Mary had the most perfect faith of anyone and so God blessed her more than all others.)

65. DID JESUS CHRIST HAVE FAITH?

No. Jesus was God Himself, the Second Person of the Blessed Trinity. The created soul of Jesus always had the vision of God. He did not need faith, for our Lord beheld God face to face within His soul.

(No. Jesus was God. He did not need faith.)

66. DID MARY SUFFER IN HER HEART WITH JESUS SUFFERING ON THE CROSS?

Yes. By compassion Mary suffered in union with Jesus. It was the sins of men that caused Jesus to suffer. God willed that His Mother should share in the pain. Mary was the one Jesus loved most. Mary's great sympathy for Jesus caused pain in her Immaculate Heart.

(Yes, when Mary saw Jesus suffering so much, it hurt her, too.)

67. WAS IT THE SINS OF MEN THAT CAUSED MARY TO SUFFER?

Yes. Just as sins caused Jesus to suffer, they also caused Mary to suffer when she saw what sin was doing to her adorable Son.

(Yes. When people sin against Jesus that hurts Mary's Immaculate Heart, too.)

68. WHAT DOES THE FOLLOWING MEAN: JESUS IS OUR MEDIATOR AND MARY IS OUR MEDIATRIX?

Jesus is our Mediator because He alone won our redemption. Jesus alone merited our salvation. He needed no other person to win for us the forgiveness of sin and sanctifying grace so as to live the life of heaven. Mary is mediatrix because she gave us Jesus and freely accepted the pain of her Son Jesus just as He suffered. Mary's sufferings depended on Jesus and received their power from Him.

(Jesus is the bridge to get to heaven. Mary helps us use that bridge well and shows us how.)

69. DID MARY THEN MERIT OUR SALVATION?

Yes, but only secondarily. The sacrifice of Jesus' death on the cross was perfect atonement (reparation). Mary joined her sufferings to those of Jesus, suffering with Him, and meriting with Him and as dependent on Him, the salvation of the whole world. In this way Mary gives grace through her Immaculate Heart.

(Yes, but Jesus won our salvation first. Mary helped Jesus.)

SUMMARY:

Mary cooperated with Jesus so perfectly that Jesus is called the Mediator and Mary is called the mediatrix. Jesus is the one necessary bridge between heaven and earth. Jesus alone merited our salvation; but in doing so, Jesus came to us through His Mother Mary and wants us also to go in Him to God through Mary. Jesus always said "yes" to His heavenly Father. In saying "yes" it was not always easy for Jesus. He had to suffer often in so doing. That made His Mother suffer, too, to see her Son suffer. Mary wanted whatever Jesus wanted so she always said "yes" with Jesus to the heavenly Father.

Although Mary was truly the Mother of God she still had to have faith. Not until Mary arrived in heaven did she see God "face to face, even as He is," as the Bible describes our seeing the Most Blessed Trinity when we get to heaven. Mary did not win us any grace of her own power, not from her own soul as the source; but Mary, by perfectly cooperating with her Son Jesus, did merit for us the same graces which Jesus *first* merited for us. Everything Jesus did, Mary made her own by willing our salvation in union with her Son.

QUESTIONS:

1. How is Jesus our brother?
2. What is sanctifying grace?
3. How did Mary do the same things Jesus did?
4. How do our sins cause Mary to suffer?
5. Who is our perfect model in Christian faith?

PRACTICE:

Ask Mary for an increase of faith. Mary will obtain faith for you from her Son. Pray often to Jesus and Mary, "I believe, Lord; help my unbelief, Mary my Mother."

8

CATHOLIC DEVOTION TO MARY
(Questions 70-76)

70. DO CHRISTIANS OTHER THAN CATHOLICS HONOR THE MOTHER OF GOD?

Yes, the Orthodox Churches, for one, have a deep devotion and honor for the Mother of God. Protestant Christians are gradually developing a devotion to God's Mother.

(Yes. Many Christians besides Catholics love and honor Mary.)

71. DO CATHOLICS ADORE MARY?

No. Only God can be adored. Jesus Christ is adored because He is God, the Second Person of the Blessed Trinity. The body and soul of Jesus are adored because the created body and soul of Jesus are one with God the Son. Catholics venerate Mary. This means that Catholics show Mary more honor than all the angels and saints.

(No. Catholics adore only God.)

72. IN WHAT DOES TRUE DEVOTION TO MARY CONSIST?

True devotion to Mary must be based on the fullness of the true Catholic faith. From true faith we are led to know the greatness of the Mother of God.

From our knowledge of Mary as the Mother and mediatrix of all graces, we are moved to love her as spiritual children and to imitate her virtues. True devotion to Mary then depends upon Jesus and her being God's Mother.

(True devotion to Mary means imitating her faith and love for Jesus. It also means loving Mary for giving us Jesus.)

73. DOES MARY MERIT GRACE FOR US NOW THAT SHE IS IN HEAVEN?

No. Mary does not now merit grace from her Son for us. Mary does intercede for us with Jesus to give us grace. This means that just as God willed to use Mary as His instrument and cooperator upon earth, now in heaven, God still holds as very powerful the prayers of His Mother for us.

(Mary does not merit for us in heaven. By her prayers she gets for us the grace we need for our souls.)

74. WHEN DID THE CATHOLIC CHURCH DECLARE MARY TO BE THE MOTHER OF GOD?

At the Council of Ephesus in 413 the Catholic Church defined it to be a doctrine of the Catholic faith that Mary is truly God's Mother. Mary is not simply the Mother of a man in whom God lives. Rather, Mary is the Mother of Jesus Who is true God and true man.

(From earliest days the Catholic Church has believed Mary was the true Mother of God.)

75. WHAT IS MEANT BY THE MARIAN CENTURY?

The 100 years from 1854 when Mary's Immaculate Conception was defined to be part of the Catholic faith, until the close of Vatican Council II, is called the Marian Century. The past century was the greatest century in the history of the Catholic Church for strengthening our understanding of Catholic faith regarding the Mother of God.

(The Marian Century means that during the past 100 years greater insights have been given us to know and love Mary better.)

76. WHY DID THE PAST CENTURY NEED SPECIAL EMPHASIS ON MARY?

People were denying Jesus Christ as true God and true man. One can better understand Jesus and the Church, Christianity itself, by understanding Mary and her role in salvation.

(We needed to know and love Mary better the past 100 years so as to live as better members of the Church.)

SUMMARY:

Devotion to Mary, the Mother of God, is as old as the Catholic Church. The early Christians began developing a devotion to God's Mother. Our own time, the past century, has been called the Marian Century because devotion to God's Mother became so strong and better understood. All true devotion to Mary, however, must always stem from Jesus Who is one with God. In other words, devotion to Mary must always be united to our love for Jesus.

Catholic devotion to Mary may take many forms. We shall see later in this catechism that expressions of our devotion to Mary may be found in such things as praying the Rosary, wearing the Brown Scapular, but always, devotion to Mary depends on the truth that she is the Mother of God. It would be an exaggeration to honor and love Mary and forget why Mary is so great and lovable. One must never separate the Mother of God from the Son of God. In fact, we should remember Mary's relationship to the entire Blessed Trinity and her special place in the Church.

QUESTIONS:

1. Why would it be wrong to adore Mary?

2. What does Mary do for us now in heaven?

3. How will our understanding Mary help us to know Jesus better?

4. What must we always remember in true devotion to Mary?

PRACTICE:

To develop a strong and true devotion to Mary, ask Jesus to help you love His Mother as He did. You could never love Mary as much as Jesus; but if you desire it, and ask for it, Jesus surely will respond to your request for the grace to love His Mother more.

9

MARY AND VATICAN II
(Questions 77-84)

77. WHAT DID VATICAN COUNCIL II (1962-1965) SAY ABOUT MARY?

The Pope and the world's Catholic bishops, meeting at the Vatican for the Second Vatican Council, spoke most beautifully about Mary. Pope John placed Vatican Council II under the special care of Mary. Vatican Council II helped Christians see better how Mary relates not only to Christ, but to the Church.

(The world's bishops and the Pope said that we should always think of Jesus and His Church when we think of Mary.)

78. WHAT SPECIAL TITLE DID POPE PAUL VI GIVE MARY AT THE SECOND VATICAN COUNCIL?

At a session of the Council when Pope Paul VI, on November 21, 1964 gave to the Catholic world the *Dogmatic Constitution on the Church* and the *Decree on Ecumenism,* he told the thousands of Council Fathers that he was proclaiming the Most Blessed Mary, *"Mother of the Church."*

(Pope Paul asked us to call Mary "Mother of the Church.")

79. WAS THE TITLE, "MOTHER OF THE CHURCH," NEW TO CHRISTIANS?

No, but the Pope said, "We wish that the Mother of God should be still more honored and invoked by the whole of Christendom through this most sweet title." He also said, "It is precisely by this title, in preference to all others, that the faithful and the Church address Mary."

(No. The Catholic Church has always known that Mary was its Mother.)

80. WHAT WAS SPECIAL ABOUT THE "TIME" IN WHICH THE POPE ASKED THE WORLD OFTEN TO CALL MARY BY THE TITLE, "MOTHER OF THE CHURCH"?

On that same day (November 21, 1964), the Pope was giving the Church a constitution on the nature of the Church, in which an entire long chapter was devoted to Mary and her role in the Church. Also, that same day the Pope was giving the world the decree on the Christian unity movement. For Christian unity it is very important that all Christians rightly understand the true role of Mary.

(When Pope Paul asked us to call Mary "Mother of the Church" he was also speaking about the Church and stated that all Christians should have one faith.)

81. DID THE POPE DO ANYTHING ELSE VERY SPECIAL AT THE COUNCIL REGARDING MARY WHEN HE GAVE THE WORLD THE DOCUMENTS ON THE CHURCH AND CHRISTIAN UNITY?

Yes. The Pope used that same occasion to tell the bishops of the world that he was renewing the consecration of the world to the Immaculate Heart of Mary. The Pope said that he was sending a golden rose to the sanctuary of Fatima. The Pope mentioned that the sanctuary of Fatima "is known and venerated throughout the entire Catholic world. In this manner we intend to entrust to the care of this heavenly Mother the entire human family, with its problems and anxieties, with its legitimate aspirations and ardent hopes."

(Yes. When the Pope gave the world more knowledge about the Church and stated that all Christians should be one in faith, he consecrated the world to the Immaculate Heart of Mary.)

82. DID VATICAN COUNCIL II SPEAK OF MARY AS MEDIATRIX?

Yes. Vatican Council II said that Mary's role as Mother began when in faith she said "yes" at the Annunciation of the angel. The Council also said her role as Mother continued beneath the cross and will last now that she has been taken up to heaven. From heaven she continues to bring us eternal salvation by her intercession. By her motherly charity Mary still cares for us upon earth until we are led to our true home in heaven. "Therefore," said the Council, underlining that this does not take away from Jesus as the one Mediator, "the Blessed Virgin is invoked by the Church under the titles of Advocate, Auxiliatrix, Adjutrix, Mediatrix."

(Yes. The Pope and world's bishops said that all grace from Christ comes to us through Mary, too.)

83. WHAT WERE SOME OF THE IMPORTANT

TIMES MARY IS MENTIONED IN THE NEW TESTAMENT?

In the New Testament Mary is shown with faith and giving her consent to the role of Jesus on these occasions: When God the Son is conceived in Mary by the Holy Spirit; when Jesus is born at Bethlehem; when the shepherds and the Magi visit the Christ Child; when the Holy Family flees into Egypt; when Jesus is offered in the temple; when Jesus is twelve years old and is found teaching the scribes and elders; when Jesus is teaching as an adult in the Gospels; when Jesus works the first public miracle at the wedding feast of Cana; when Jesus especially praised His Mother because having heard the Word of God, she pondered it in her heart; when Mary is with Jesus in His sufferings and stands under the cross on the hill of Calvary; when Mary is with the disciples after Jesus ascends into heaven and stays with them praying in the upper room; when Mary is with the Apostles on Pentecost Sunday, the day the Holy Spirit descends upon the young Church in the form of fire.

(Mary is mentioned at the most important times in the New Testament from beginning to end.)

84. WHAT DID JESUS MEAN AS HE SPOKE THESE WORDS WHILE DYING ON THE CROSS: "WOMAN, THIS IS YOUR SON. . . . THIS IS YOUR MOTHER"?

The Apostle John writes about this in his Gospel. John was the particular disciple whom Jesus loved in a special way. Jesus' dying thoughts were of His Mother. John from that moment on made a place for Mary in his home. The Apostle John represented the entire human race. Jesus was speaking as the Redeemer of the world in all that He said from the cross. By those words Jesus was giving Mary to us as our spiritual Mother.

(When Jesus was dying on the cross He gave Mary to us as our Mother, too, when He said, "This is your Mother.")

SUMMARY:

For four years, 1962-1965, the Catholic bishops from all over the world gathered at the Vatican in Rome. Vatican City is where the Pope lives. The Pope is the visible head of the Church and the chief representative of Jesus on earth. For four years the bishops met under the authority of the Pope. Their meeting was called "Vatican Council II." That Council gave the Church sixteen documents. One of those documents was on the nature of the Church. The last chapter by the world's bishops on the nature of the Church was on Mary, the Mother of God, and her role in salvation. The bishops spoke at length and beautifully about Mary. The Second Vatican Council asked Catholics to continue their devotion to Mary in relationship to Jesus Christ and the Church.

During the Council the Pope met with about 2,300 bishops before him. It was then that the Pope asked all Catholics to call upon Mary often under her title, "Mother of the Church." At the same time and at the same Council, the Pope reconsecrated the entire world to the Immaculate Heart of Mary. The Pope said that he was sending a golden rose to the sanctuary of Fatima, Portugal. The Pope would travel to Fatima later to pray there himself to the Mother of God.

QUESTIONS:

1. What was Vatican Council II?
2. How is Mary the Mother of the Church?
3. What did the Pope say about Fatima at Vatican Council II?
4. Does Mary's work as mediatrix take away from Jesus as the one Mediator? Explain answer.
5. Name as many occasions as you can when Mary is mentioned in the Bible.

PRACTICE:

Often when you are praying, use that very special title, "Mother of the Church."

10

THE BODY OF MARY AND THE BODY OF CHRIST
(Questions 85-97)

85. HOW IS MARY OUR MOTHER?

Mary is our spiritual Mother in the order of grace. Jesus is the source of all grace. Mary is therefore the Mother of grace. Jesus is the Vine and we are the branches. Jesus is the Head of the Church. Mary is the Mother of the Head of the Church which is Christ's Mystical Body. By being Mother of the Head or Vine, Mary is Mother of the members, the branches. This makes Mary the Mother of the Church.

(Mary is our Mother of grace. She gave us Jesus Who merited all grace for us.)

86. WHERE IS THE BODY OF MARY NOW?

The body of Mary is now in heaven together with her soul. This is a truth of Catholic faith.

(The body of Mary is in heaven now. It never turned to dust.)

87. HOW DO WE KNOW THAT MARY IS IN HEAVEN IN BOTH HER BODY AND SOUL?

We know that Mary is in heaven in both body and soul because the Catholic Church teaches it. The

Church is the Mystical Body of Jesus and the Holy Spirit guides the Catholic Church so that it teaches only true faith. Jesus said to His Church that He would give it the Holy Spirit, the Spirit of Truth, to keep it in the truth. Jesus said to the Church, "He who hears you, hears Me."

(We know that the body and soul of Mary are in heaven because the Church that Jesus placed upon this earth teaches it.)

88. WHEN DID THE CHURCH FIRST BEGIN TO BELIEVE THAT MARY'S BODY WAS TAKEN INTO HEAVEN?

The Catholic Church has always believed that Mary's body was assumed into heaven.

(The Apostles believed that Mary was taken up into heaven.)

89. WHEN DID THE CATHOLIC CHURCH DEFINE ITS FAITH REGARDING THE ASSUMPTION OF MARY'S BODY INTO HEAVEN?

On November 1, 1950, Pope Pius XII defined what was already the faith of the Catholic Church with these words: "By the authority of our Lord Jesus Christ, of the Blessed Apostles Peter and Paul, and by Our Own authority, We pronounce, declare, and define as divinely revealed dogma: The Immaculate Mother of God, Mary ever Virgin, after her life on earth, was assumed, body and soul to the glory of heaven."

(The Catholic Church in 1950 said all Catholics must believe Mary's body is in heaven.)

90. MUST CATHOLICS BELIEVE IN MARY'S IMMACULATE CONCEPTION AND IN HER ASSUMPTION?

Yes. Catholics must believe in Mary's Immaculate Conception and in her bodily assumption into heaven. If any refused to believe these truths of faith, they would not in fact be Catholics. If a Catholic deliberately rejects these or any other truths of the Catholic faith which have been solemnly defined by the Church, he would not be a real Catholic. Catholics must believe in the fullness of true faith, not only in part of it.

(Yes. Catholics must believe in the Immaculate Conception because we must believe everything the Catholic Church teaches.)

91. DID MARY EVER RECEIVE HOLY COMMUNION?

Most probably. John, the beloved disciple, was the favorite Apostle of Jesus. The Bible says that after Jesus' death on the cross, John took Mary into his own home. John surely obeyed Jesus' command to celebrate the Holy Eucharist, the Mass. Mary then surely received her loving Savior and Son Whom she could hardly bear to be separated from, such as when he was twelve years old and she and Joseph lost Him.

(More than likely. Jesus commanded us to eat His body and drink His blood in Holy Communion. As the perfect Christian Mary surely wanted to do that.)

92. WAS MARY PRESENT AT THE LAST SUPPER WHEN THE FIRST MASS WAS OFFERED?

The Bible does not mention it.

(We do not know for sure.)

93. WHY IS MARY CALLED "OUR LADY OF THE HOLY EUCHARIST"?

The Blessed Virgin Mary is called "Our Lady of the Holy Eucharist" because the Jesus Who is really present in this great and most holy sacrament is the same Jesus born of Mary, nursed and reared by Mary, Whom she taught. The body and blood of Jesus was taken from the body of Mary. The same Word of God, the Son, Who was made flesh in Mary by the power of the Holy Spirit, is the same Jesus we receive in Holy Communion. The very same Jesus Who lives in the tabernacles of our Catholic churches, is the same Jesus Who once lived in the sweet womb of Mary for nine months.

(Mary is called "Our Lady of the Holy Eucharist" because she first gave us the same living Jesus we now receive in this holy sacrament.)

94. WAS JESUS BORN LIKE ALL OTHER CHILDREN?

Jesus had no human father. The Baby Jesus lived beneath Mary's Immaculate Heart for nine months like other babies before birth. When it came time for Jesus to be born, the Baby Jesus passed from the womb of Mary into her arms.

(No. Jesus came into the world from Mary's body by a special power of God.)

95. WAS JESUS CONCEIVED ONLY IN MARY'S WOMB?

No. Mary gave consent in her mind and heart. The early Fathers of the Church used to say, "Jesus was conceived in Mary's heart before He was conceived in her womb."

(No. Mary first loved Jesus in her heart. Then Jesus lived in her body, too.)

96. WHAT DOES IT MEAN, "JESUS WAS CONCEIVED IN MARY'S HEART"?

The heart of Mary means the whole person of Mary. It means her understanding and especially her will. Mary freely willed to become the Mother of Jesus. She knew that by becoming Mother of the Man of Sorrows, Jesus Christ, she would also become the Mother of Sorrows. It was Mary's heart, her intellect and will, which first made the decision to say "yes." Then Jesus became flesh in her womb.

(That Jesus was conceived in Mary's heart means that Mary knew the Word of God in her mind so well that Jesus lived in her heart by love even before He became a little baby boy in her holy body.)

97. WHAT DOES MARY BECOMING A MOTHER NINE MONTHS BEFORE JESUS WAS BORN SAY ABOUT ABORTION?

Abortion is the sin of murder whereby a baby is killed before birth when it is still in its mother's womb. When we pray the Hail Mary we say, "Blessed is the fruit of thy womb, Jesus." Mary went to visit her cousin immediately after the angel told her she was to be the Mother of the Son of God. Elizabeth greeted Mary with the words, "Mother of my Lord," showing that Mary was a mother right after conceiving Jesus. A woman becomes a mother about nine months before her child is born and so did Mary.

(From the moment Mary said "yes" to the angel she was a mother. Mothers in the world today who have an abortion are really killing live babies.)

SUMMARY:

There are many ways we can think of the body of Christ. The Bible calls the Church "the Body of Christ." All God's people with Jesus make up the Mystical Body of Christ. Then there is the body of Christ, born of Mary, which died on the cross, rose from the dead, ascended and is now in heaven as the glorified body of Christ. Finally, there is the *eucharistic* body of Christ. This is the body of Jesus in the Most Blessed Sacrament, the same body, blood, soul and divinity of our Savior Jesus Christ Whom we receive in Holy Communion. In all three cases, it is the body of Jesus but under different ways of existing.

The body of Jesus is in heaven now. So is the body of His Mother Mary in heaven now. Jesus and Mary are in heaven as king and queen in both their bodies and their souls. How wonderful it must have been for the Blessed Virgin Mary to receive Jesus in Holy Communion from the Apostle John after Jesus had ascended into heaven. The same Jesus she carried in her womb for nine months, nursed, clothed, cared for in so many ways, that same Child Who was her Son and her God, she could still adore in the Most Blessed Sacrament and receive in Holy Communion.

Just as Jesus and Mary in the Bible and in the life of the Church are inseparable, so in heaven they are inseparable. They are both there, body and soul.

QUESTIONS:

1. What are the three ways of speaking of the body of Christ?

2. Did Mary receive Holy Communion?

3. Is the body of Jesus we receive in Holy Communion the same Jesus Mary carried in her body before Jesus was born?

4. How does Mary's life in the Bible tell us that abortion is killing real human life?

5. How is Mary the Mother of the Church?

PRACTICE:

Whenever you receive Jesus in Holy Communion, or when you come before the tabernacle in church, remember that in this sacrament our Lord and God, Jesus Christ, is really and truly present. Adore and love Him then as Mary would.

11

MARY, MODEL OF PRAYER
(Questions 98-104)

98. WHY IS MARY OUR MODEL OF THE CHURCH WHEN WE WORSHIP?

Mary is our perfect example when we come to divine worship, for Mary of all members of the Church was most perfect in faith, charity and union with Christ. These dispositions of Mary's heart are needed when the Church, associated with Jesus our Lord and through Him, worships God the Father.

(Mary is our model when we worship because Mary worshiped most perfectly.)

99. GIVE SOME EXAMPLES OF MARY RECEIVING THE WORD OF GOD WITH DEEP FAITH.

Mary's great faith prepared her to become the Mother of God. It was Mary's faith which was the cause of her blessedness. The Gospel says, "Blessed is she who believed that the promise made her by the Lord would be fulfilled." Mary's faith then played a great part in God becoming man in Jesus so as to save the world. With faith Mary pondered in her heart the events of the infancy of Jesus and all He taught as an adult.

(Mary believed the angel that she was to become the Mother of God. Mary often thought in her heart with faith about things in the life of Jesus.)

100. GIVE SOME EXAMPLES OF MARY AS A MODEL OF PRAYER.

Mary's prayer is called the "Magnificat" (Luke 1:46-55) which she prayed when she visited Elizabeth. This prayer of Mary has become the prayer of the Church all over the world for all times.

At Cana Mary prayed to her Son Jesus so that He worked His first public miracle. By Mary's prayer at Cana the disciples' faith in Jesus was strengthened (John 2:1-12).

Mary is last seen in the Bible with the Apostles "joined in continuous prayer" (Acts 1:14). Here Mary is at prayer with the early Church. Now that Mary is assumed into heaven, she still prays for and with the Church in the Communion of Saints.

(The Bible tells us of Mary's prayers. She praised God for doing great things for her. She asked Jesus to change water into wine. She prayed with the Apostles after Jesus went to heaven.)

101. HOW IS MARY COMPARED TO THE SACRAMENT OF BAPTISM?

The power of the Holy Spirit in Mary brought forth Jesus, the Head of the Church. The power of the Holy Spirit in the Sacrament of Baptism brings forth the believer in Jesus. Mary carried the life of Jesus in her womb. The Church witnesses the life of Jesus in its members by the waters of baptism. Christ's members and the Church's members are all one and the same.

(The Holy Spirit worked in Mary to give us Jesus and the Holy Spirit works in baptism to make us like Jesus.)

102. HOW IS MARY THE PERFECT MODEL OF THE CHURCH MAKING OFFERINGS?

At every holy sacrifice of the Mass we offer Jesus to God the Father. We also offer ourselves by faith in Jesus. Mary first offered Jesus in the temple (Luke 2:22-35). The prophet Simeon took the Child Jesus, looked at Mary and said, "Your own soul a sword shall pierce." This came true on Calvary. Beneath the cross Mary was offering Jesus to God the Father for the salvation of the world.

(Mary offered Jesus to God the Father again and again, especially at the foot of the cross. We do the same at every Mass.)

103. HOW DOES MARY JOIN IN THE OFFERING OF THE HOLY EUCHARIST?

Jesus gave the Church the Holy Eucharist to perpetuate down through the centuries the selfsame sacrifice of the cross. Whenever the Church offers the Eucharist (the Mass), it joins the saints in heaven in the offering, especially the Blessed Virgin. The Church imitates Mary's burning charity and unshakable faith in offering Jesus at the sacrifice of the Mass.

(Just as Mary offered Jesus at the foot of the cross, so today, when she sees the Mass being offered, Mary, from heaven, makes that offering again.)

104. HOW IS MARY A PERFECT TEACHER OF THE SPIRITUAL LIFE?

Christians, even when they are children, look to Mary to imitate her worship of God. Mary always said "yes" to God. She always did God's will in perfect faith and love. Mary's whole life was centered on Jesus. She offered what was most dear to her, Jesus, to God the Father. The life of Mary teaches us how to live as perfect Christians.

(Mary is the perfect teacher of how to live like Jesus because she herself lived like Jesus.)

SUMMARY:

The Church is the community of God's people who have faith. The Church is most perfectly realized when it gathers in worship with the bishop. The Bible tells us of Mary, the Woman of Faith, "joined in continuous prayer" with the Apostles who were the first bishops of the Church. The more perfect one's faith and love, the more perfect is the prayer joined to Jesus. No Christian or member of the Church had a greater faith or greater love than the Mother of the Church.

Two chief parts of the sacrifice of the Mass, which is the highest form of adoration in the Church, is the Liturgy of the Word of God (which is the first part of the Mass), and the Liturgy of the Eucharist (which is the latter part of the Mass). Now Mary is the perfect model of the first part, for she with her great faith is shown in the Bible pondering the Word of God in her heart. That is what we should do during the first part of the Mass. The holy sacrifice of the Mass perpetuates the same offering of Jesus' sacrifice of the cross. On the hill of Calvary, Mary first offered in perfect faith her Son to God the Father as she stood beneath the cross. We, too, like Mary, should offer the sacrifice of Jesus at every Mass. Every time

Mass is offered Mary still makes the same offering from heaven.

QUESTIONS:

1. What was Mary's heart like when she came to prayer?

2. Name the two general parts of the Mass and show how Mary is our model in both parts.

3. As a perfect teacher or catechist what does Mary teach us?

4. What are the things which Mary and baptism do which are alike?

PRACTICE:

When you pray, especially at the holy sacrifice of the Mass, join your heart to the Immaculate Heart of Mary so as to pray and worship as she did.

12

THE CHURCH,
THE ROSARY AND MARY
(Questions 105-113)

105. COULD THE CHURCH EXIST WITHOUT MARY?

Not as we know it. Love for the Church is love for Mary, and vice versa, since the one cannot exist without the other. The Church was united in the Upper Room with Mary, the Mother of Jesus, and with His brethren. The Church cannot be referred to unless it includes Mary, the Mother of our Lord, together with His brethren. Mary is the Mother of the Church. The Church is the family of God, the people of God, the kingdom of God and the Mystical Body of Christ, all of which are images of the Church. Of all this, Mary is the spiritual Mother. God Himself decided that Christ would not exist without Mary; therefore neither could His Church.

(No. Without Mary there would be no Church for then there would be no Jesus.)

106. WAS MARY PRESENT AT THE BIRTHDAY OF THE CHURCH?

Yes. Pentecost is the birthday of the Church. The Church as the Mystical Body of Christ, Vine and branches, has Head, Soul and members. Jesus Christ is the Head. The Holy Spirit is the Soul of the

Church. We as God's people are the members. The birth of the Church was complete only at Pentecost when the Holy Spirit came down upon the early Church in the form of tongues of fire. Mary, the Mother of the Church, was present at the birthday of the Church. The Holy Spirit overshadowed Mary when the Head of the Church was conceived. When the *whole* Church was born on Pentecost, the Holy Spirit overshadowed Mary again.

(Yes. Mary, the Mother of the Church, was there when the Holy Spirit came down in the form of tongues of fire.)

107. DOES THE BLESSED VIRGIN MARY HAVE AN IMPORTANT PLACE IN THE NEW LITURGY OR DIVINE WORSHIP OF THE CATHOLIC CHURCH?

Yes. Pope Paul VI in writing on true devotion to the Blessed Virgin Mary said: "If one studies the history of Christian worship, in fact, one notes that both in the East and in the West, the highest and purest expressions of devotion to the Blessed Virgin have sprung from the liturgy or have been incorporated into it." This is true to the present day.

(Yes. There are many feasts of Mary in the Church's Year of Worship. Also, Mary is mentioned at every holy Mass.)

108. WHAT DID VATICAN COUNCIL II SAY ABOUT PRACTICES AND EXERCISES OF DEVOTION TOWARD MARY?

Vatican Council II charged that such devotions toward Mary were to continue to be treasured by the

Church as recommended by the teaching authority of the Church in the course of the centuries (Chapter 8, *Lumen Gentium*).

(The Pope and bishops of the world have said that Catholics will continue to have devotions to Mary as Catholics have had for centuries.)

109. DID THE TEACHING AUTHORITY OF THE CHURCH STATE EXACTLY WHAT THESE DEVOTIONS OF THE CENTURIES WERE THAT WERE TO BE CONTINUED IN THE CHURCH?

Yes, and more than once has the Pope declared examples of what Vatican Council II meant. On February 2, 1965, two months and two days after declaring that time-tested devotions were to stay, the Pope said: ". . . Ever hold in great esteem the practices and exercises of the devotion to the most blessed Virgin which have been recommended for centuries by the Magisterium of the Church. And among them we judge well to recall especially the Marian Rosary and the religious use of the Scapular of Mount Carmel."

(The Pope said that the Church still strongly recommends the praying of the Rosary and the wearing of Mary's Brown Scapular.)

110. WHAT DID THE POPE SAY TO ALL THE BISHOPS OF THE WORLD ABOUT THE RIGHT ORDERING OF DEVOTION TO MARY AND CATHOLIC DEVOTIONS?

The Pope especially asked for the continued use of the Angelus and the Rosary. Pope Paul VI on many occasions since the Council has recommended the frequent recitation of the Rosary. (Cf. *Marialis Cultus.*)

(The Pope asked that Catholics pray not only the Rosary but the Angelus.)

111. WHAT DID POPE PAUL VI SAY ABOUT THE NATURE OF THE ROSARY IN HIS APOSTOLIC EXHORTATION TO THE WORLD'S BISHOPS ON DEVOTION TO MARY?

The Pope said that the Rosary meditated considers the chief saving events in the life of Christ. The Pope praised the division of the mysteries of the Rosary into three parts. He said that the fifteen mysteries in the Joyful, Sorrowful and Glorious Mysteries is a correct order of the facts and reflects the plan of the first way the faith was made known to the world. (Cf. *Marialis Cultus.*)

(The Pope told the bishops of the world that when we pray the Joyful, Sorrowful and Glorious Mysteries of the Rosary we think of the chief truths of our Catholic faith.)

112. WHAT IS MEANT BY THE SAYING, THE ROSARY IS "THE COMPENDIUM OF THE ENTIRE GOSPEL," AS USED BY POPES (PIUS XII, PAUL VI)?

It means that the content of faith in the Gospel, which is the written Word of God, inspired the Rosary. It means the Rosary is a Gospel prayer. Meditation on the fifteen mysteries of the Rosary means pondering in our hearts, as did Mary the perfect Christian and Mother of the Church, the chief saving events that will bring us to our true home, heaven.

The proper praying of the Rosary will keep us safe in the true faith.

(The holy Rosary is like another Gospel, a little Bible of true faith.)

113. WHAT IS THE PROPER WAY TO PRAY THE ROSARY?

Pope Paul VI *(Marialis Cultus)* said that without meditation on the mysteries of the Rosary "the Rosary is a body without a soul." The soul of the Rosary is thinking on the Joyful, Sorrowful or Glorious Mysteries while one prays the litany-like succession of Hail Marys. We should "meditate on the mysteries of the Lord's life as seen through the eyes of her who was closest to the Lord." The Hail Marys become as soft music in the background of our thoughts, while the saving events of Jesus' life in the foreground are the soul of the Rosary.

(The most proper way to pray the Rosary is to think of the big events or mysteries of Jesus' life while we say the Hail Marys.)

SUMMARY:

When the bishops of the world met at the Second Vatican Council (1962-1965) and discussed the nature of the Church, they decided that Mary can best be understood only as part of the Church. Therefore, they wrote at length and most beautifully about Mary at the same time they were teaching the world about the Church. Mary is the Mother of the Church, present at all stages of the Church's development as it came from God. Mary's own word brought the Head of the Church, Jesus, to this earth. That was when she answered "yes" to the angel. Mary is so close to and inseparable from Jesus Christ that the liturgy (worship) of the Church year has many important feasts of Mary.

True devotion to Mary is a mark of true Christianity in its fullness. Devotion to Mary can take many forms, but the Church told us at Vatican II that devotions to Mary which the Church has recommended for centuries would continue to be encouraged. Pope Paul, shortly after the Council, told us clearly that a high place among these recommended devotions should be given to the Rosary and the Scapular of Mt. Carmel. Later he also included the prayer called the Angelus.

Pope Paul VI wrote in 1974 to all the bishops of the world instructing the whole Church on the proper way to pray the Rosary. He encouraged meditation on the fifteen mysteries of the Rosary as divided into Joyful, Sorrowful and Glorious. This proper way of praying the Rosary would then keep us mindful of the true faith as taught by the Gospels.

QUESTIONS:

1. Why can Mary and the Church be understood best only when we consider both of them together?

2. Of what does Mary's presence at Pentecost remind us?

3. Point out how the fifteen mysteries of the Rosary take in all the chief events of salvation.

4. What did Vatican Council II say about devotions to Mary?

5. Which Catholic devotions to Mary has the Pope especially recommended?

PRACTICE:

Say the Angelus each day. Imitate Mary's heart in pondering the events of Jesus' life as you pray the decades of the Rosary.

13

THE LITURGY AND THE ROSARY
(Questions 114-120)

114. WHAT IS THE LITURGY OF THE CHURCH?

Liturgy means the official worship of God by the Church through such actions as the sacrifice of the Mass, the sacraments and praying of the Divine Office. Sacramentals are also connected with the liturgy.

(When the Catholic Church worships God, as in the Mass and sacraments, that is called liturgy.)

115. IS THE ROSARY ONE OF THE CELEBRATIONS OF THE LITURGY OF THE CHURCH?

"Liturgical celebrations and the pious practice of the Rosary must be neither set in opposition to one another nor considered as being identical. . . . The Rosary is a practice of piety which easily harmonizes with the liturgy. . . . The Rosary . . . draws its motivating force from the liturgy and leads naturally back to it, if practiced in conformity with its original inspiration. It does not however become part of the liturgy." These words of Pope Paul VI (*Marialis Cultus*) remind us that meditation on the Gospel mysteries, which is the proper way to pray the Rosary, keeps the Rosary in harmony with the liturgy.

(No. The Rosary is not liturgy but is something

like it. The Rosary helps us to prepare to take part in the holy Mass better.)

116. SHOULD THE ROSARY BE PRAYED DURING THE MASS?

No. Pope Paul VI said, "Meditation on the mysteries of the Rosary . . . can be an excellent preparation for the celebration of those same mysteries in the liturgical action and can also become a continuing echo thereof. However, it is a mistake to recite the Rosary during the celebration of the liturgy, though unfortunately this practice still persists here and there" (*Marialis Cultus*).

(No. The Rosary should not be said during Mass. The Rosary is better said before Mass or at any other time of the day or night.)

117. WHAT IS THE BODY OF THE ROSARY?

The body of the Rosary is the litany-like recitation of the Hail Marys. The Hail Mary comes from the Angel Gabriel's greeting to the Virgin and from Elizabeth's greeting. This first half of the Hail Mary is in the Bible. The second part is a prayer of the Church. A total of 150 Hail Marys make up the entire Rosary in its three cycles. The 150 prayers represent the 150 Psalms of David in the Bible. One of the three cycles gives rise to the Rosary of fifty Hail Marys as we know it. The Our Father and the Glory Be to the Father are also part of the body of the Rosary. (Cf. *Marialis Cultus*.)

(The body of the Rosary is the different memorized prayers we say on the different beads.)

118. MAY ANY OF THE FATIMA PRAYERS BE ADDED TO THE ROSARY?

Yes. A decree from Rome (February 4, 1956) authorized the recitation of the special Fatima prayer after each decade of the Rosary in private and public devotions (Office of Indulgences, 878:56). The prayer is: "O my Jesus, forgive us; save us from the fire of hell; lead all souls to heaven, especially those in greatest need (of thy mercy)."

(Yes. At Fatima Mary gave us a beautiful little prayer to say after each ten Hail Marys and Glory Be.)

119. WHAT IS THE BEST PRAYER FOR THE FAMILY IN OUR HOMES?

"There is no doubt that, after the celebration of the Liturgy of the Hours, the high point which family prayer can reach, the Rosary should be considered as one of the best and most efficacious prayers in common that the Christian family is invited to recite" (*Marialis Cultus*).

(If families do not say a long prayer called the Divine Office, the next best prayer to pray in our homes is the holy Rosary.)

120. SHOULD CATHOLICS DEVOTED TO MARY, TO HER ROSARY AND SCAPULAR, USE PRESSURE TO GET OTHERS TO PRACTICE THESE DEVOTIONS?

No. Such would do harm to Mary's beautiful prayer and distort the true devotion to God's Mother and approved practices. Pope Paul VI said it this way, in outlining the high regard the Apostolic See (Vatican) has for the Rosary of the Blessed Virgin:

"We desire at the same time to recommend that this very worthy devotion should not be propagated in a way that is too one-sided or exclusive. The Rosary is an excellent prayer, but the faithful should feel serenely free in its regard. They should be drawn to its calm recitation by its intrinsic appeal."

(No. Neither Mary nor the Popes force the Rosary on us, although they encourage this devotion. We should tell others how beautiful the Rosary is so that they will want to pray it.)

SUMMARY:

When the liturgy of the Catholic Church is being conducted, the very Person of Jesus Christ is present and is acting. We can understand this especially during the sacrifice of the Mass and the administration of the Sacraments. In the liturgy the members of Christ are joined to the very Person of our Lord Jesus Christ Who is the chief Priest of the liturgy. Jesus uses other men of the Church to carry out such perfect worship, especially ordained men in Holy Orders. When it is true liturgy of the Catholic Church the adoration given the Blessed Trinity is no more or less powerful than if you were actually present with Jesus as He lived 2,000 years ago upon this earth and adored God in His human body as at the Last Supper or while hanging on the cross. The liturgy is Jesus present, acting, worshiping in His holy Church today.

The Rosary is not liturgy in the strict sense. There are many things about the Rosary, when properly prayed, that prepare us better to offer the liturgy of the Mass or receive the Sacraments. Pondering the Word of God, that is, the fifteen mysteries of the Rosary, surely prepares our hearts to offer the liturgy with greater faith and love.

It is unfortunate that some devoted to Mary do harm to her cause by putting undue pressure on others to pray the Rosary or act as if the Rosary were of equal importance with the liturgy of the Church. Both are important but they are not equal in importance. When the Rosary is properly understood, when the soul of the Rosary is prayed as well as the mechanics or memorized prayers, then the Rosary has a beauty in itself which will attract others to pray as Mary did. A person who feels superior because he prays the Rosary daily, and condemns others who do not, is not acting as the Woman of Faith and of charity which typifies the Mother of God as presented in the Bible.

QUESTIONS:

1. Who is the chief priest whenever true liturgy is conducted?

2. Explain both the soul and the body of the Rosary.

3. Is a person spending an hour in prayer in his home conducting liturgy? Explain.

PRACTICE:

Pray the Rosary daily as the Church recommends. Remember that the Rosary prayed properly, is an excellent preparation for participation in the sacrifice of the Mass.

14

OUR LADY'S GARMENT — THE BROWN SCAPULAR
(Questions 121-136)

121. IS THE BROWN SCAPULAR OF OUR LADY OF MT. CARMEL AN APPROVED SACRAMENTAL OF THE CHURCH?

Yes, not only is it approved, the Brown Scapular is strongly recommended.

(Yes. Many Popes have told us how beautiful it is to wear the Brown Scapular.)

122. WHERE DID THE BROWN SCAPULAR OF MT. CARMEL ORIGINATE?

The beginnings of the Brown Scapular have a long history. It began to develop even in the Old Testament when God's people were awaiting the coming of Jesus. A group of hermits who believed themselves to be the spiritual sons of Elias the Prophet lived on Mt. Carmel in Palestine. They pondered the Word of God in their hearts. When Jesus founded the Church these hermits also developed a deep devotion to the Mother of God. They became known as "The Brothers of Our Lady of Mt. Carmel." The Saracen invasion forced them to leave Mt. Carmel. They came to the West.

St. Simon Stock became the new superior general of the Carmelite Order in 1246 at Aylesford, England. His Order was having so many problems he feared it would end. Our Blessed Mother appeared to St. Simon Stock giving him the scapular of the Order. She said: "This shall be a sign to you and to all Carmelites: Whosoever dies wearing this shall not suffer eternal fire."

In time, the devotion to Our Lady of Mt. Carmel and her Brown Scapular spread throughout the entire world and won the approval of the Church.

(The idea of the Brown Scapular comes from heaven. The Blessed Virgin Mary first gave it to St. Simon Stock. When Popes learned of it they wanted all Catholics to wear it to show Mary how much we love her.)

123. DOES THE CHURCH APPROVE OF PRIVATE REVELATIONS AS GIVING US NEW OR DIFFERENT CATHOLIC FAITH?

No. The Catholic Church has never and will never approve of any new revelations that add to or take away from the Catholic faith. The faith of the Catholic Church as given us by heaven, was completed by the time of the death of the last Apostle. Our understanding of that faith may grow. Revelations given to certain special people through the centuries may remind us of the faith, or help us understand better what is already the Catholic faith. The faith may develop, but it does not change. Only our understanding of the faith may change, by increasing.

(No. When Mary or any of the angels or saints appears to somebody here on earth, they never tell us any new Catholic faith. The Church sometimes approves of appearances of persons from heaven when it agrees with our Catholic faith.)

124. ON WHAT FAITH OF THE CHURCH DOES THE BROWN SCAPULAR DEVOTION DEPEND?

The Brown Scapular devotion stems from our faith in the fact that Mary is the Mother of God and the spiritual Mother of all members of the Church. The Brown Scapular, when worn with devotion and love for Mary, is a sign of one's consecration to God's Mother. It has no power within itself. A piece of cloth does not bring our salvation. The devotion of the Brown Scapular depends upon the power of Mary's intercession for those who wear it.

(Catholics believe in the power of Mary's prayers for them if they wear her Brown Scapular.)

125. HAS OUR BLESSED MOTHER EVER REVEALED THE BROWN SCAPULAR TO OTHERS BESIDES ST. SIMON STOCK?

Yes, to Pope John XXII and, in 1917, to the three Fatima children. Pope John XXII is said to have issued a document (papal bull) March 3, 1322, about the Brown Scapular and the Blessed Virgin appearing to him and promising a great reward to those who wore the Brown Scapular under certain conditions.

(Yes. Even after Mary gave the Brown Scapular to St. Simon she has appeared to others showing them the same scapular.)

126. WHAT WAS THE GREAT REWARD, AND THE TWO CONDITIONS REQUIRED FOR IT, ABOUT WHICH POPE JOHN XXII WROTE?

The great reward was a promise given by the

Blessed Virgin to Pope John XXII that those who wore the Brown Scapular, lived a life of chastity (purity) according to their state in life, and recited the Office of Our Lady, would through her intercession be released from purgatory on the first Saturday after death. This is called the Sabbatine Privilege. Nine different Popes, besides Pope John XXII, have spoken of the Sabbatine Privilege and reconfirmed the teaching.

(If Catholics wear the Brown Scapular, are pure in thought and action, and say the daily Rosary, they may believe Mary will take them out of purgatory soon after death.)

127. MUST ONE SAY THE OFFICE OF THE BLESSED VIRGIN TO GAIN THE SABBATINE PRIVILEGE?

Yes, unless one has permission from an authorized priest to substitute the daily Rosary. Members of the Blue Army of Our Lady of Fatima are given the privilege to say the daily Rosary in place of the Office.

(We may say the Rosary each day while wearing the Brown Scapular and believe we will go to heaven soon after death.)

128. MUST ONE WHO WEARS THE BROWN SCAPULAR ALSO SAY THE DAILY ROSARY OR DESIRE TO OBTAIN THE SABBATINE PRIVILEGE?

No. When our Lady gave her promise of assured salvation, "Whosoever dies clothed in this shall not suffer eternal fire," she did not mention that the daily

Rosary was also necessary to the promise. Ideally, the Rosary should be prayed daily and we are already bound to live a life of chastity according to our state in life as ordinary Christians.

(No. One may choose only to wear the Brown Scapular. Mary wants us to also say her Rosary each day.)

129. DOES THE SCAPULAR MEDAL HAVE THE SAME PROMISE ATTACHED AS THAT OF THE BROWN CLOTH SCAPULAR?

Although the Holy See has issued a regulation that a medal may be substituted for the scapular, it must be remembered that our Blessed Mother herself did not give us the scapular medal. She gave the cloth to St. Simon Stock and in our own century at Fatima, Mary held up the cloth, not the medal. We may belong to the Confraternity of the Carmelites through wearing the medal. This point is important. The reward of assured salvation, attached to the Brown Scapular and making this devotion of Our Lady of Mt. Carmel primary among devotions to Mary, is not mentioned in the papal decree on the medal. Pope Pius X who made the scapular medal decree said: "I did not intend that the scapular medal should supplant (take the place of) the Brown Scapular in Europe and America. I wear the cloth. Let us never take it off."

(No. We know that Mary's promise concerned only the Brown Scapular.)

130. WHAT IS THE THIRD ORDER OF CARMEL?

People who belong to the Third Order of Carmel are people who live in the world, or apart from community living with priests, brothers and sisters of the Carmelite Orders, yet share in a special way in all the holy Masses, prayers and good works of the Carmelites throughout the world. One who is only enrolled in the cloth and wears the scapular belongs to the Confraternity of Carmel. To belong to the Third Order of Carmel, it is further required to seek Christian perfection according to the spirit of the Carmelite Order. They pledge themselves to certain prayers and religious practices.

(Catholics who wear the Brown Scapular and are properly enrolled in it belong to the Confraternity of Mt. Carmel. To belong to the Third Order of Carmel, other prayers are required.)

131. MUST ONE BE ENROLLED IN THE BROWN CLOTH SCAPULAR TO BELONG TO THE CONFRATERNITY OF MT. CARMEL?

Yes. Either a priest or someone else properly authorized to do so, must enroll us formally in the Brown Cloth Scapular. Just wearing the scapular is not enough. We must also have been enrolled. No special prayers are required to belong to the Confraternity of Mt. Carmel. One must, however, wear the scapular with faith and love.

(Yes. Before wearing the scapular we should be enrolled in the Brown Cloth Scapular.)

132. WHERE DOES THE POWER PROMISED IN

CONNECTION WITH THE SCAPULAR ORIGINATE?

The power associated with the Brown Scapular comes from the intercessory power of the Mother of God, the prayers of the Church and our own faith and love for Jesus Christ and Mary, His holy Mother.

(The power of the Brown Scapular comes from the prayers of Mary and the Church for those who wear it.)

133. WHAT INTERPRETATION HAS SISTER LUCIA, FATIMA SEER OF OUR OWN CENTURY, GIVEN TO THE BLESSED VIRGIN PRESENTING THE BROWN SCAPULAR IN 1917?

Sister Lucia was asked why our Lady held the scapular in her hand in the final vision at Fatima. She answered: "Because she wants everyone to wear the scapular." Then Sister Lucia added: ". . . Because it is our sign of consecration to her Immaculate Heart."

(Sister Lucia of Fatima said that Mary held up the Brown Scapular in our own times because Mary still wants us to wear it.)

134. WHICH POPE SPOKE OF THE BROWN SCAPULAR AS A SIGN OF CONSECRATION TO MARY'S IMMACULATE HEART?

Pope Pius XII said of the Brown Scapular, "May it be to them a sign of their consecration to the Most Sacred Heart of the Immaculate Virgin." Sister Lucia has reechoed the Pope's words and said, "The scapular and the Rosary are inseparable."

(Pope Pius XII said if we wear the scapular it is a sign that we consecrate ourselves to Mary.)

135. HOW IS THE SCAPULAR A SIGN OF CONSE-CRATION TO THE IMMACULATE HEART OF MARY?

A good mother provides clothing for her children. Mary as our Mother has given us this garment. When we wear it we are saying to her, "I accept you as my Mother and I want to please your heart." By baptism we are adopted children of God. The scapular is a sign that we are adopted children of Mary by our own free choice.

(Mary gave us the clothing of the Brown Scapular. When we wear it, like good children, we say, "I want to be your child. I want you for my Mother.")

136. IS THERE ROOM FOR ABUSE IN THE WEAR-ING OF THE BROWN SCAPULAR?

If one were to wear the Brown Scapular and then think he could live a sinful life and still be saved, that would indeed be an abuse. Popes have warned people against abusing Mary's great promise. One, while wearing the scapular, must live in love and faith in Christ and try to avoid sin and have a continuous devotion to God's Mother.

(Yes. It would be wrong to wear the scapular and think we did not have to live a good Catholic life.)

SUMMARY:

The Brown Scapular of Mt. Carmel is one of those Catholic devotions to Mary which was included in the Second Vatican Council's statement that practices and exercises of devotion to Mary "be treasured as recommended by the teaching authority of the Church in the course of centuries. . . ." Very early in

Christianity, devotion to our Lady began and out of it grew the wearing of the Brown Scapular as a badge and sign that we are Mary's spiritual children. The scapular is a sign of our consecration to Mary's Immaculate Heart. The power, connected with the scapular, does not come from the cloth but from the prayers of the Church, the intercessory power of Mary's prayers and our own love and faith in Jesus and God's Mother.

One who thinks the promises connected with wearing the Brown Scapular are too great is underestimating the power of God and the power of the prayers of God's Mother. All baptized Christians are sons of God and are also spiritual children of Mary. Those who belong to the Confraternity of Mt. Carmel, by being enrolled in the Brown Scapular and wearing it, identify themselves in a special way as spiritual children of Mary, consecrated to her Immacualte Heart. An abuse of the scapular would be to think one could wear it and then live a careless Christian life. Such a one would doubtlessly grow weak in the faith and love which inspire one to wear the scapular in the first place.

The centuries of repeated recommendations by Popes and the repeated approved communications from heaven involving Our Lady of Mt. Carmel should leave little doubt that the devout wearing of the scapular is pleasing to the Church and the Mother of the Church.

QUESTIONS:

1. Does the cloth of the Brown Scapular have power in itself to help our salvation? Explain.

2. How does one become a member of the Confraternity of Mt. Carmel?

3. What are the spiritual advantages of belonging to Carmel's Third Order?

4. What does the devout wearing of the Brown Scapular especially signify?

5. What would be an abuse of wearing the Brown Scapular?

PRACTICE:

Ask a priest to enroll you in the Brown Scapular if you are not yet enrolled. Then, kiss your scapular each day remembering you are Mary's child, close to her heart.

15

THE IMMACULATE HEART OF MARY
(Questions 137-140)

137. WHAT IS MEANT BY DEVOTION TO THE IMMACULATE HEART OF MARY?

The Immaculate Heart of Mary stands for her whole person, but especially for the love she has for us in Christ. Mary loves God first with her heart. She loves us, her spiritual children, with the same love as we are joined to Jesus by baptism. Devotion to her heart means joining our will to Mary's will. Mary loved God's Word and meditated on it. In imitation of her heart, we, too, should meditate on the Word of God. Jesus should be the center of our lives and will be if we are devoted to Mary's heart.

(Devotion to the Immaculate Heart of Mary means we love Mary as she first loved us. It means, too, we try to imitate Mary in her perfect way of loving and believing.)

138. IS MARY'S HEART WOUNDED IN THE SAME WAY AS THE HEART OF JESUS IS WOUNDED?

Mary's heart is wounded indirectly whenever the heart of her Son is wounded by sin. What hurts Jesus, hurts Mary. These two hearts are inseparable. Mary suffered at the foot of the cross, her heart pierced by a sword, as the prophet Simeon had foretold. By compassion Mary experienced the sufferings of Jesus. Sin committed today against the Sacred Heart of Jesus is also committed against the Immaculate Heart of Mary who is the Mother of the Church. Her heart is rightly described as sorrowful and immaculate.

(Mary's heart feels the pain of the sins committed against Jesus Whom she loves so much. What hurts Jesus hurts His Mother, too.)

139. HAS THE CHURCH APPROVED OF DEVOTION TO THE SORROWFUL AND IMMACULATE HEART OF MARY?

The Church both approves and encourages devotion to the Sorrowful and Immaculate Heart of Mary. Pope Pius XII consecrated the world to the Immaculate Heart of Mary on October 31, 1942. Pope Paul VI, on November 21, 1964, addressing the third session of Vatican Council II, in the presence of the bishops of the world, renewed the consecration of the world to the Immaculate Heart of Mary. At the same time he gave the Catholic world the Council's *Dogmatic Constitution on the Church* and the *Decree on Ecumenism* (Christian unity). At the same time he asked us to call upon Mary by her title, "Mother of the Church." Still another thing the Pope did at that session of the Council was to announce that he was sending a golden rose to Fatima. This was approval of the sanctuary of Fatima, where Mary asked for devotion to her Sorrowful and Immaculate Heart.

(Yes. The Church wants us to love the Immaculate Heart of Mary. The Church wants us to remember how our sins cause sorrow to Mary's heart.)

140. IS THERE ANY ORGANIZATION SANCTIONED BY THE CHURCH FOR PROMOTING THE MESSAGE OF OUR LADY OF FATIMA?

Yes. On May 24, 1975, the Holy Year, a document was presented to Bishop John Venancio of Fatima, the International President of the Blue Army, by Archbishop Neves of the Council of the Laity. The document officially informed the Blue Army that it had been inscribed by the Holy See among the international organizations of the Church. The purpose of the Blue Army is to spread throughout the world the message of Fatima which Pope Pius XII called a "reaffirmation of the Gospels." The Blue Army seeks to have people both know and *live* the Fatima message. For children and youth up to eighteen years of age there is a Blue Army of Our Lady of Fatima Cadets.

(Yes. The Blue Army of Our Lady of Fatima is approved by the Church to teach us what Mary said at Fatima in our own century. There is a Blue Army Cadet division for children and young Catholics.)

SUMMARY:

Devotion to the Immaculate Heart of Mary is the foundation of all other devotions to Mary. The love of the Immaculate Heart of God's Mother is the very soul and spirit of all other devotions to Mary. To use an example: Without charity, all other Christian virtues would remain without value. In the same way, all Marian devotions are without value unless joined to devotion to Mary's Immaculate Heart.

The message of the heart is the message of love. Today there is a sad lack of love between peoples, even between fellow Christians. The example of the motherly love of Mary is God's way of teaching us how to unite ourselves to Jesus Christ. Mary always leads us to Jesus. The love of the Immaculate Heart leads to the love of the Sacred Heart of Jesus. If devotion to the Immaculate Heart of Mary becomes strong in the world, the world will be saved, for it will find in the heart, in the love of God's Mother, the very love of God.

By showing us the love of the Immaculate Heart of Mary, God is showing us a way that is completely merciful. Certainly the love of the heart of Mary is not more powerful than the love of the Sacred Heart for us; but the love of the Woman of Faith, by God's merciful designs, teaches us how to live a perfect Christian life. God's Mother really loves us. She is the Mother of the Church and she loves and is concerned about her children. The love of the Immaculate Heart can best teach us how to love her Son and one another and return to Jesus the love He has for us.

QUESTIONS:

1. Are the loves of the Immaculate Heart and the Sacred Heart in competition with each other? Give the reason for your answer.

2. How is Mary's Immaculate Heart wounded by our sins?

3. What does it mean, the hearts of Jesus and Mary are inseparable?

PRACTICE:

Each day express in your heart love for the Immaculate Heart of Mary. Then remember that God is very pleased when you love His Mother. A good short prayer is: "Immaculate heart of Mary, be my salvation." This means Mary leads you to the Savior.

16

MARY IN OUR TIMES
(Questions 141-149)

141. DOES THE CATHOLIC CHURCH APPROVE OF THE USE OF STATUES AND VARIOUS IMAGES?

Yes. Vatican Council II in charging that practices and exercises of devotion toward Mary be treasured as recommended by the Church for centuries said this about religious images: "Those decrees issued in earlier times regarding the veneration of images of Christ, the Blessed Virgin and the saints, (are to) be religiously observed" (*Lumen Gentium*).

(Yes. The Catholic Church approves of the use of statues and images of Jesus, Mary, angels and the saints. We must, however, always understand that these things do not have power in themselves.)

142. DOES THE CATHOLIC CHURCH BELIEVE THAT POWER COMES FROM STATUES OF JESUS, MARY OR THE SAINTS?

No. The Catholic Church, however, through her bishops and priests, does bless such religious objects. The material object has no religious power. The power comes from the prayers of the Church. They may serve to uplift our minds to God. The love and faith they inspire in our souls may be an occasion of grace.

(No. Religious objects merely help us to pray.)

143. WHAT IS MEANT BY THE PILGRIM VIRGIN STATUE?

Pilgrim Virgin Statues have traveled around the world for many years. They take their inspiration from the apparitions of Our Lady of Fatima in 1917. There are different kinds of Pilgrim Virgin Statues: international, national, diocesan and parish Pilgrim Virgin Statues. The purpose is to have them travel to different areas to renew in the hearts of people the requests made by Our Lady at Fatima. Rightly used and understood, these Pilgrim Virgin Statues inspire devotion related to Jesus Christ, the Source of all truth, sanctity and piety.

(A Pilgrim Virgin Statue is one that is moved from place to place. As the statue moves around, it helps people to know and love God and Mary better.)

144. HAVE POPES APPROVED OF THE PILGRIM VIRGIN STATUES?

Yes. On June 4, 1951 Pope Pius XII directly referred to Our Lady of Fatima and the Pilgrim Virgin as he talked to pilgrims. The Pilgrim Virgin Statue has visited the Vatican at different times and has always been received kindly by the Popes. Pope Pius XII blessed an Immaculate Heart Pilgrim Virgin Statue (January 5, 1954) to visit different areas of the world. This same Pope spoke of the Pilgrim Virgin Statue as "the messenger of her royalty."

(Yes. Different Popes have themselves blessed and shown respect for Pilgrim Virgin Statues.)

145. DOES OUR BLESSED MOTHER'S RELA-

TIONSHIP TO US CONCERN ONLY HER YEARS ON EARTH?

No. Mary is not simply a woman of history as Jesus is not merely a God-Man of history. Both Jesus and Mary live now in heaven in their bodies and souls. As king and queen in heaven, their concern for us continues at this very moment and always will. The appearance of the Sacred Heart of Jesus to St. Margaret Mary in 1675 and the appearance of the Immaculate Heart of Mary at Fatima in our own century, tell us that Jesus and Mary know us, love us and care for us, now.

(No. Mary as a good Mother, now that she is in heaven, watches over and cares for us constantly.)

146. DOES FATIMA HAVE ANY SPECIAL SIGNIFICANCE FOR THE WORLD?

Yes. Communism, which has as its goal world domination, comes out of Russia. Our Blessed Mother said at Fatima that unless her requests were granted, "Russia will spread her errors throughout the world, bringing new wars and persecution of the Church; the good will be martyred and the Holy Father will have much to suffer; certain nations will be annihilated. But in the end my Immaculate Heart will triumph. . . ." The small gold ball one sees on the Pilgrim Virgin Statues of Fatima is a reminder that the message of Fatima is for the world.

(Yes. Mary came to Fatima, not only for Portugal but for the whole world. If we do the things Our Lady of Fatima asked, Communism will not take over the world.)

147. HAVE POPES POINTED OUT THE WORLD-WIDE IMPORTANCE OF FATIMA?

Yes. Pope Paul VI at the worldwide gathering of bishops at Vatican II spoke of Fatima, relating the worldwide significance of Mary and Fatima. Pope Paul VI personally visited Fatima as a humble pilgrim on May 13, 1967. Earlier, on May 13, 1946, a personal representative of our Holy Father went to the sanctuary of Fatima and there crowned Our Lady of Fatima "Queen of the World." On October 13, 1951, Pope Pius XII talked by radio to a million pilgrims assembled in the Cova da Iria at Fatima and said: "This time it is not . . . only the angel of the Lord, it is the Queen of Angels herself who goes forth in her miraculous images from the most celebrated shrines of Christians and chiefly from this sanctuary of Fatima — where heaven permitted us to crown her *Regina Mundi* (Queen of the World) — to make jubilee visits to all her dominions. . . ."

(The Pope at Fatima crowned the statue of Our Lady of Fatima as Queen of the World. Pope Paul VI went to Fatima and before cameras and writers from the whole world, presented Sister Lucia to everyone.)

148. HAVE THE BISHOPS OF THE UNITED STATES SHOWN THEIR APPROVAL OF FATIMA?

Yes. Our American bishops in their Marian pastoral letter, *Behold Your Mother, Woman of Faith* (November 21, 1973), spoke of "the authenticated appearances of our Lady and their influence on Catholic devotion." They added: "Best known of the 20th century appearances of the Mother of the Lord is that at Fatima, in 1917."

(Yes. The bishops of the United States said that Fatima was a true appearance of Mary.)

149. WHAT HAVE THE APPROVED APPEARANCES OF MARY UPON THIS EARTH ALL HAD IN COMMON?

Those appearances of Mary upon this earth which the Church has approved have the following points in common: 1) Mary has always called us back to union with God and her Son, Jesus Christ; 2) Mary has always repeated what was already the faith of the Catholic Church; and 3) Mary always calls us to prayer and sacrifice in reparation for sin.

(When Mary has come to earth she has asked for prayer and penance so as to live close to Jesus in His Church.)

SUMMARY:

Mary has not forgotten us. Mary is very much a part of our times. As the Mother of the Church, Mary is concerned about her spiritual children in every century. If anything, our age, called "the Marian age," means that Mary, God's holy Mother, has manifested her love for the Church even more so to meet the needs of our sinful world.

In Paris, in 1830, Mary made herself known to St. Catherine Labouré as the Immaculate Mother who sheds rays of grace from her hands upon men of the whole world. (In her great purity she is seen as the mediatrix of all graces.) Then in 1846 on a mountain of La Salette in southeast France the Blessed Virgin appeared to two little shepherds, Melanie Calvot and Maximin Giraud. At La Salette Mary is seen in tears, weeping for all those who ignore God and offend Him by sin. In Lourdes, in 1858, our Lady appeared in this southern town of France to fourteen-year-old Bernadette Soubirous eighteen times at the nearby grotto of Massabielle. When Bernadette asked her name, the Lady said, "I am the Immaculate Conception." She gave a message for all: "Pray and do penance for the conversion of the world." The waters that have flowed at the rate of 27,000 gallons a day started with a trickle when Bernadette dug into the floor of the cave at the bidding of the vision. Our Lady smiled much at Lourdes.

In 1917 at Fatima, Portugal, our Lady appeared to three small children: Jacinta, about seven, Francisco, nine, and Lucia, hardly ten years of age. Our Lady again asked for prayer and sacrifices. Our Lady predicted wars if men did not turn from their sins. The errors of Russia, usually understood as Communism, would spread over the world if men did not turn to prayer and to reparation. Our Lady smiled but once briefly at Fatima when she told the children, "God is pleased with your sacrifices." At Fatima it was announced by heaven, "God wishes to establish devotion to the Immaculate Heart of Mary in the world and to save it by this means." The life of Jacinta reveals her strong devotion to the Immaculate Heart. The Fatima messages can be summed up in the word, "Reparation."

QUESTIONS:

1. What is the proper Catholic use of statues?
2. How does God's Mother show interest in souls in our times?

3. How is Fatima of interest to the world and not just Portugal?

PRACTICE:

Read a good book on Fatima. Develop an awareness that Mary loves you now.

17

MARY, MODEL OF REPARATION
(Questions 150-163)

150. WHAT ARE THE FOUR KINDS OF PRAYER?

The four kinds or purposes of prayer can be remembered by the word ARTS: each letter stands for the beginning letter in a kind of prayer. Thus: 1) Adoration — to adore God; 2) Reparation — to make satisfaction to God; 3) Thanksgiving — to thank God; and 4) Supplication — to ask God for what we need. The best prayer has these four elements in the same order as ARTS. Most people begin prayer by asking God for something, but this comes last in the right kind of prayer.

(As above.)

151. WHAT DOES REPARATION MEAN?

Reparation is one of the four kinds of prayer. Reparation is making satisfaction or atonement to God for sins committed against God by ourselves and others. Every sin is an offense against God and justice demands that we make satisfaction to God. Reparation is repairing the damage done to God. For example, if we deliberately break a window, to make satisfaction we repair the window or pay to have it fixed. Jesus paid for our sins, that is, He made satisfaction for them by shedding His precious blood on the cross. We can pray or do things in a spirit of reparation. Each time we say an Act of Contrition we are making reparation to God.

(Reparation means to make up to God for sins against Him by praying or doing good things for the love of Jesus.)

152. CAN WE MAKE REPARATION FOR ONE AN-OTHER?

Yes, and we should. Just as Jesus made satisfaction for all of us, we can offer prayers and sacrifices to God in reparation to Him for the sins of the whole world. We are members of the Mystical Body (the Catholic Church). We can help one another.

(Yes. By our prayers and sacrifices we can make up to God for the sins of others.)

153. CAN WE WIN THE CONVERSION OF SIN-NERS?

Yes. In the approved apparitions of Mary here on earth, this is one of the things Mary has said. We are to pray and offer satisfaction for sinners so that their souls may be saved through the merits of Jesus Christ. It is still Jesus Who saves. When Mary prays, it is therefore still Jesus Who saves.

(Yes. By our prayers and sacrifices we can win from Jesus graces to save souls.)

154. HOW IS MARY OUR PERFECT MODEL IN REPARATION?

As the woman who was the perfect model of faith and the perfect Christian when she lived on earth, she must also be perfect in fulfilling that purpose of prayer, called satisfaction or reparation. Her entire life was one of reparation. She first offered her life to a state of virginity for the love of God. She constantly gave of herself in perfect faith and love. That is the image the Bible gives us of Mary. She was always doing the will of God most perfectly in everything she did. The high point of all this was when she stood at the foot of the cross and offered her Son to the heavenly Father as Jesus died for the sins of the world. Mary was suffering and dying in her heart as Jesus was in His body. Mary offered all her sorrows to God in reparation for the sins of the world and in union with her Son.

(Mary always did the will of God in all things. She offered everything to God for souls.)

155. WHY IS THE APPROVED MESSAGE OF FATIMA SAID TO BE SUMMARIZED IN DEVOTION TO THE SORROWFUL AND IMMACULATE HEART OF MARY?

Mary's Sorrowful Heart reminds us of reparation which is so important to a good Catholic life and the message of Fatima. Devotion to Mary's Immaculate Heart reminds us of the perfect life of love, faith and service which Mary lived in a constant spirit of prayer. Mary's heart was always centered on her Son Jesus. Devotion to the Sorrowful and Immaculate Heart of the Mother of the Church then, if lived in our daily lives, will be a living of the Word of God as taught us in the Gospels.

(At Fatima our Lady taught us to make sacrifices for the sins which wound the hearts of Jesus and Mary. At Fatima our Lady called us to love as she does.)

156. WOULD THE CATHOLIC CHURCH BE DE-STROYED IF CATHOLICS NO LONGER PRACTICED REP-ARATION?

Yes. If any Christian fails to see the need for rep-aration, he has lost the sense of sin. If one does not realize sin as an offense against God, he will see no need to make reparation. Jesus said that unless we do penance, we shall all likewise perish. Also, "Unless you take up your cross daily and follow me, you are not worthy of me." We cannot be disciples of Jesus without the spirit of penance. We have the promise of Jesus that the Catholic Church could never be com-pletely destroyed. "I will be with you all days, until the consummation of the world. . . . Upon this rock I will build my Church and the gates of hell shall never prevail against it."

(God has promised us that the Catholic Church will never be destroyed. But if any Catholic does not do any penance, or make any reparation, he can lose the true faith.)

157. WHEN WE MAKE REPARATION TO THE SACRED HEART OF JESUS, WE ARE MAKING REPARA-TION TO GOD HIMSELF. BUT WHY SHOULD WE MAKE REPARATION TO MARY'S IMMACULATE HEART?

First, remember this. When you make repara-tion to Mary's Immaculate Heart you are making reparation to the Sacred Heart. These two hearts are inseparable. Reparation is always directed finally to God Himself. In the Communion of Saints, in the Church, Mary is our Mother and when we sin we fail not only God, but our Mother. What hurts the Son, hurts the Mother. What pleases the Mother, pleases the Son. Peace with God's Mother is peace with her Son and God Himself. We can then understand the expression that God has confided the peace of the world to the Immaculate Heart of His Mother. It is the way of mercy and love.

(When we love Mary, we also love Jesus. Mary always leads us to Jesus. Mary is hurt by our sins because they hurt Jesus. If we make reparation to please Mary, that pleases Jesus, too.)

158. WHAT IS THE DIFFERENCE BETWEEN PENANCE AND REPARATION?

Penance is often considered making satisfaction for one's personal sins. Reparation, while including satisfaction for one's own sins, is much wider. We make satisfaction to God for the sins of the world and for the conversion of sinners.

(We do penance to make up for our own sins. We make reparation for sins of the whole world.)

159. WHAT IS THE BEST KIND OF REPARATION?

While anything which is not sin can be offered to God to atone for sin, the best form of reparation is before and in union with the Most Blessed Sacrament. This includes first of all the Mass, then adoring Jesus in the Most Blessed Sacrament in a spirit of reparation. This is called eucharistic reparation. Everything we do during the day should be a living of the Mass.

(The best kind of reparation is participation in the sacrifice of the Mass. We should also adore the real

presence of Jesus in the Most Blessed Sacrament of the tabernacle.)

160. WHY WOULD GOD AND HIS CHURCH EMPHASIZE DEVOTION TO THE IMMACULATE HEART OF MARY? IS NOT DEVOTION TO THE SACRED HEART OF JESUS ENOUGH?

At the present moment, it is the will of God that devotion to the Immaculate Heart of Mary is most useful for our spiritual life. The message of the heart is the message of love. Today people of the world, including Catholics, too often separate themselves from each other and God by lacking a spirit of love. Therefore, God shows us the perfect way a Christian loves by showing us the heart of His Mother.

(God Himself wants us to love His Mother. We are happy when people love our mother. Jesus is happy when we love His Mother.)

161. DOES GOD WANTING DEVOTION TO THE IMMACULATE HEART OF MARY MEAN THAT MARY'S HEART IS MORE POWERFUL THAN THE HEART OF JESUS?

No. Jesus is God and must be all-powerful as God. By teaching us through the Church (and through Fatima) devotion to the Immaculate Heart of Mary, God wishes to show us a way that is completely merciful. It is like saying, "They have not listened to the heart of My Son as they should; now I will send the heart of My Mother." The Mother leads us to her Son. Making known to us devotion to the Immaculate Heart through the Church, is heaven being merciful to us again to draw us to heaven.

110

(No. Jesus is God and is all-powerful. It is the love and mercy of God that share with us the love of His Mother.)

162. WHAT IS COMMUNISM?

Communism, as is usually defined, means the errors of Russia which have been spreading over the world. Real Communists do not believe in God. Communism wrongly teaches that there is no life after death. It denies the immortal human soul. Communistic governments take away all freedoms from people when and where they get complete control. One is then not permitted to own private property. The state becomes the people's god. Under Communism, people are not free to worship God as they want. Since men do not have souls and there is no God, according to Communism, this terrible system of forced government sees nothing wrong with killing people when it wants to for its own purposes. It also believes there are no moral laws given man by heaven. Nothing is a sin. The only sin for Communists would be not to serve the state. Communism wants to take over the world. Communism will not succeed if people live good Christian lives.

(Communism is an evil kind of government that takes away the freedom and rights of people. Communists do not believe in God or in man's immortal soul.)

163. MUST WE BELIEVE IN FATIMA?

If one speaks of the strict obligation to believe in the same way that Catholics must believe defined doctrines of the Church, then we are not obliged to believe in Fatima. However, the Fatima messages are already part of the Catholic faith. If we speak of a certain obligation to follow the spirit which moves the Church at every moment of time, then it is not true to say that we may ignore Fatima. At this moment of the Church the Holy Spirit is working in the Church through Fatima.

If we want to have the sense of the Church, then the Church has approved Fatima as a great means of the Christian life. No danger threatens the faith and Catholic discipline when Fatima is properly understood. Fatima teaches what the Church teaches.

(We do not have to believe in Fatima like we do in the Bible or the doctrines of the Catholic Church. We believe in Fatima only because the Church says it teaches what is already Catholic faith.)

SUMMARY:

Reparation is one of the four kinds of prayer. Reparation means offering sacrifices to God to satisfy for the sins of mankind. Jesus made reparation for the entire world by the sacrifice of His death on the cross. When Jesus redeemed the world He was making reparation for the world's sins. Mary co-merited with Jesus. It was Jesus Who saved as Redeemer. Mary saved only through her prayer and suffering in union with Jesus. Mary made the sufferings of Jesus her own. She suffered in her heart what Jesus also suffered in soul and body. Mary made reparation for the whole world, but she was dependent on and in union with her Son Jesus to accomplish it.

Sometimes we see images of Mary's heart pierced with thorns. It reminds us of the Sacred Heart of Jesus pierced with thorns which represent the sins of men. As sin offends the Sacred Heart of Jesus, so sin offends the Immaculate Heart of His Mother. Mary loves both Jesus and the members of His Church. Jesus is the invisible Head of the Church and Mary is the Mother of the Church. In all Jesus offered in reparation as Head, Mary also offered as Mother. Jesus' perfect act of reparation is perpetuated at every sacrifice of the Mass. Just as Mary joined in the offering at the foot of the cross on that first Good Friday, the Immaculate Heart of Mary, now from heaven, joins the Sacred Heart of Jesus every time Jesus, as high Priest, offers the Mass through His Church on earth.

QUESTIONS:

1. How can we remember the four elements of perfect prayer?

2. When did Mary offer her greatest act of reparation?

3. What are some ways we can make reparation for others?

4. Can we help save souls? Explain answer.

5. What would happen to your country if atheistic Communism took over?

PRACTICE:

Perform some act of sacrifice (reparation) each day for the conversion of sinners. When making a sacrifice in reparation say some prayer such as: "O my Jesus, this is for love of You, for the conversion of sinners and in reparation for sins committed against the Immaculate Heart of Mary."

18

EASTERN-RITE CHRISTIANS AND THE MOTHER OF GOD
(Questions 164–171)

164. WHO ARE EASTERN-RITE CATHOLICS?

Eastern-Rite Catholics are Catholics who hold the same beliefs, morality and purpose as Western-Rite or Roman-Rite Catholics. They have the same faith but different customs, especially in the manner of worship. Eastern-Rite Catholics are very dear to the Pope, and they recognize him as the supreme bishop of the world and visible head of the Church on earth. Eastern-Rite Catholics are every bit as Catholic as Western-Rite Catholics. They are in union with the Holy See, that is, with the Pope. There are some twenty-two other rites in the Catholic Church, although the greatest portion belong to the Roman Rite. (In the U.S., the Eastern Rites have eight dioceses or eparchies which were established by the Pope for the government of Eastern Catholics according to their respective laws and liturgical traditions.)

The word "rite" means the outward expression in worship of one's internal belief. This especially includes differences in the eucharistic sacrifice which is commonly called the sacrifice of the Mass.

Eastern-Rite Catholics have a profound sense of veneration for God's Mother.

(Eastern-Rite Catholics are Catholics who believe the Pope is the visible head of the Church. They love

God's Mother greatly. Their customs of worship only are different.)

165. WHAT IS THE BYZANTINE RITE OF WORSHIP?

It is the expression of worship used by many Eastern-Rite Catholics in union with the Pope. It takes its name from Constantinople, which was once called Byzantium. Oftentimes it is called the "Greek Rite" because of its Greek beginnings. The Byzantine Rite is the second most widely used liturgy after the Roman Rite. It is used by many million Eastern Orthodox Christians and by several million Catholic Byzantines.

(The Byzantine Rite of worship is a very beautiful way of offering the holy sacrifice of the Mass and the Sacraments. The ceremonies are different from those practiced by Roman Catholics, but the basic rite has the same powers of Jesus that are present. Byzantine-Rite Catholics believe in the authority of the Pope and are just as much Catholic as Roman Catholics.)

166. ARE EASTERN-RITE CATHOLICS THE SAME AS ORTHODOX CHRISTIANS?

No. There are close to 200 million non-Catholics who use the same Eastern Rites as those who are in union with the Pope. The majority of them are behind the Iron Curtain where these Christians are victims of persecution under Communistic governments. Byzantines who are separated from the Pope are called "Orthodox" although the name Orthodox is not really an accurate title. The Holy See calls them "Dissidents." In most points of belief the Orthodox have faith very similar to that of Catholics with the exception that they do not recognize the powers of the Pope. Orthodox Christians have a deep devotion also to the Mother of God.

(No. Eastern-Rite Catholics accept the Pope as the visible head of the Church upon earth. Orthodox Christians do not accept the Pope as the visible head of the Church.)

167. ARE THE SACRAMENTS OF THE ORTHODOX VALID?

For the most part, yes. They have a valid priesthood. Their priests really have the powers of changing bread and wine into the body and blood of Jesus Christ, and of forgiving sins in the name of Jesus Christ. There are a number of groups among them, however, which call themselves Orthodox, but are not really united to the Orthodox Church and whose sacraments are not recognized by the Catholic Church. Among the traditional Orthodox, such as the large national groups of Greeks, Russians, Serbians, Rumanians, Albanians, Syrians, etc., it is believed that they have a true priesthood. This is why the Orthodox are so much closer to us than Protestant Christians. The Apostolic chain was broken for the hundreds of Protestant denominations. When they broke from the ancient Catholic Church they did not have true bishops with real powers which Jesus Christ gave to the first Apostles. Therefore, without true bishops the Protestants could not ordain true priests with the powers Jesus gave the first Apostles. When the Orthodox broke from the Catholic Church through the Great Schism of 1054, they kept their true bishops. Therefore, Orthodox bishops and priests still have the powers of the Sacraments. We should pray for their complete return to union with our Holy Father, the Pope.

(The Sacraments of the Orthodox are valid Sacraments. Orthodox priests really have the powers of Jesus in the Sacraments just like Roman and Eastern-Rite Catholic priests. When the Orthodox left the Catholic Church they kept their truly ordained bishops. Protestants did not have true bishops to ordain their ministers and so Protestant Christians do not have the powers of the Sacraments except Baptism and Marriage.)

168. DO EASTERN-RITE CHRISTIANS USE STATUES?

No. They use icons. Some Eastern-Rite Catholic Churches have introduced statues, but usually they have preferred icons for religious symbols. The icon is often placed on a stand before the altar. The faithful venerate it often with a kiss as they enter the Church.

(Eastern-Rite Christians use icons instead of statues.)

169. WHAT IS AN ICON?

An icon is a painting of Jesus Christ, our Lady, or our Lady with the Christ Child. It also may be of some saint. The painting is on wood in the special Byzantine style that brings out the mystical nature or spirituality of the persons represented. They are very beautiful and sometimes richly decorated as in the case of the icon of Our Lady of Kazan. Eastern-Rite

Catholics show a great reverence for icons in their churches and in their homes. When these people come into church, instead of genuflecting in reverence to the real presence of Jesus Christ in the Most Blessed Sacrament, they make a profound bow and the Sign of the Cross. Then they kiss one of the icons.

(Icons are painted religious art on wood. Eastern-Rite Christians honor them highly.)

170. WHAT IS THE ICON OF OUR LADY OF KAZAN?

It is an icon which is a central point of the Communist revolution against God. The Basilica of Our Lady of Kazan was destroyed in Moscow after the Communists took over the country. This was an attempt to "prove" that "God does not exist." What was once her basilica in Leningrad was made the center of a worldwide movement against belief in God.

For some years after the Communist revolution in Russia it was thought that the precious icon of Our Lady of Kazan had been destroyed. Then it mysteriously appeared in a castle in England. Scholars studied it and determined it was the icon of Our Lady of Kazan. The Blue Army of Our Lady of Fatima redeemed this icon which in monetary value is worth millions. In reality, however, an icon cannot be valued in money because Eastern-Rite Christians as well as Western-Rite Christians venerate this icon greatly.

The icon of Our Lady of Kazan is in the possession of the international organization of the Blue Army of Our Lady of Fatima at Fatima. When the Christians of Russia again have freedom and Communism no longer rules Russia, the Blue Army will return to the Russian Christians this famous centuries-old icon. The Orthodox of Russia for countless generations considered it a miraculous image.

(The icon of Our Lady of Kazan is a most valuable and precious icon. It was honored by the Christians of Russia for many centuries. The Communists destroyed the Church built in her honor in Russia, but the icon was salvaged. It now belongs to the Blue Army of Our Lady of Fatima. When Christians get their religious freedom in Russia, the Blue Army will give back to Russian Christians their icon of Our Lady of Kazan.)

171. WHAT SPECIAL PLACE WILL THE BYZANTINE EASTERN-RITE CATHOLICS HAVE IN THE CONVERSION OF RUSSIA?

Our Lady of Fatima mentioned Russia by name in the apparition of July, 1917. Our Blessed Lady of Fatima was reported to have said that if men do not stop offending God there would be war, persecution of the Church and the Holy Father. The Blessed Lady of Fatima asked for the consecration of Russia to her Immaculate Heart. She said, "If my wishes are fulfilled, Russia will be converted and there will be peace. If not, Russia will spread her errors throughout the world, promoting wars and persecution of the Church. The good will be martyred, the Holy Father will have much to suffer, and various nations will be annihilated. But in the end, my Immaculate Heart will triumph. The Holy Father will consecrate Russia to me and it will be converted, and a time of peace will be conceded to the world. . . ."

The above words are a part of the approved apparition at Fatima, Portugal, in 1917. At the international headquarters for the Blue Army of Our Lady of Fatima which is now in 110 countries of the world, there is a Byzantine chapel where the sacred liturgy of the Mass is offered daily in the Byzantine-Catholic Rite, which is so close to the Russian Rite. Each day the Mass and prayers are offered for the conversion of Russia.

Pope Urban VIII once directed these words to the Catholics of the Byzantine-Slavonic Rite. "In you, I place my hope of converting the East. The Holy See does not regard the Byzantine Rite as an ancient relic or museum piece that must be coddled until it disintegrates. The Byzantine Rite has a great mission; it must not only be preserved, it must be developed and revitalized, so that in the fullness of time it may give the lie to the propaganda that poisoned the minds and hearts of millions against the Holy See."

The Byzantine-Rite Catholics have kept the true faith for centuries although they were once separated before 1595. Just as when they came back into union with the Holy See (the Pope), so, too, when Russia is converted and recognizes the Pope as the visible head of the Church on earth, Russia will be able to keep its beautiful rite which is almost identical to the Byzantine-Catholic Rite. The Byzantine Rite is considered a bridge between Rome and Russia.

Eastern-Rite Christians have a profound veneration for the Mother of God. The Mother of the Church and the Mother of Unity through her intercession will bring her children into one fold under one Shepherd.

(Byzantine-Rite Catholics have worship ceremo-

nies almost the same as Russian-Orthodox Christians.
Our Lady of Fatima promised that some day Russia
will be converted. Then Byzantine-Rite Catholics will
be a bridge to unite the Catholics who accept the au-
thority of the Pope with the Christians of Russia.)

SUMMARY:

The Roman Catholic Church had its beginning
in the eastern part of the world. As history marched
on, it moved to the western part of the world. Gradually the Christians of the Eastern world had customs
of worship with more ceremony than Catholics of the
Western world. In the year 330 A.D., Constantine the
Great had the capital of the Roman Empire moved
from Rome to a little town in the East known as
Byzantium. For almost a thousand years East and
West lived in peace, recognizing the Pope of Rome as
the visible head of the Church.

In 1054 the Great Schism took place, separating
the East from the Catholics who recognized the Pope
at Rome as the chief authority of the Church Jesus
Himself established. There was much pride and poli-
tics causing these divisions rather than deep faith and
love for God. The forces of evil were successful in
dividing Christians whereas Jesus had prayed that
His followers would always be one.

There were several attempts to join Eastern and
Western Christians. From 1595 to 1700, millions of
separated Eastern Christians returned to the unity of
the Church and recognized the Pope as the visible
head. They are every bit as Catholic as are Roman
Catholics of the Western Rite. Those Eastern-Rite
Christians who have not returned to unity with the

ancient Church are known as the Orthodox. The Orthodox do not recognize the Pope as the visible head of the Church. The Orthodox do, however, have external methods of worship very similar to Byzantine-Rite Catholics. They differ somewhat on doctrines but do have a true priesthood with the powers of the Sacraments.

Our Lady of Fatima in July of 1917 promised that someday Russia would be converted. The Byzantine-Rite Catholics will be a strong visible symbol to the Orthodox that they will be welcomed back into unity with the Pope and Roman Catholics while still being able to keep their beautiful forms of worship.

QUESTIONS:

1. Does the Catholic Church have only one approved form of worship?

2. What is the difference between Eastern-Rite Catholics and Orthodox Christians?

3. How can the Byzantine-Rite Catholics help in the conversion of Russia?

PRACTICE:

Pray every day to Our Lady of Kazan for the conversion of Russia.

19

CONSECRATION TO MARY
(Questions 172-176)

172. WHAT IS MEANT BY CONSECRATION TO MARY?

The word consecration means to make something sacred by setting it aside for the service of God. People and things can be consecrated. Consecration to Mary means giving ourselves to Jesus Christ through the Immaculate Heart of His Mother. Consecration to Mary's Immaculate Heart is really at the same time consecration to the Sacred Heart of Jesus. One who is consecrated to Mary's heart understands and lives the faith in Mary as the mediatrix of all graces. As God came to us in Jesus through Mary, we go back to God in Jesus through Mary. Jesus still saves. Mary intercedes.

(Consecration to Mary means going to Jesus through the love of His Mother.)

173. WHAT IS MEANT BY TOTAL CONSECRATION TO MARY?

Total consecration to Mary, according to St. Louis de Montfort, is to be taken very seriously and requires many weeks of study and prayerful preparation. It requires casting off the spirit of the world. It means giving up the desires of the flesh, the eyes and the pride of life. It is a real desire and effort to lead a more perfect Christian life. One strives to attain a knowledge of self at the feet of Mary. One gives up self so as to live in union with Jesus. Finally, one tries to have a greater knowledge of Jesus Christ. One goes to Mary to know Jesus better and to think and live the Christlike life. One works to live a Christian life and love our Lord as Mary did.

When one is totally consecrated to Mary, he or she gives everything into Mary's hands to do as her Immaculate Heart desires. All our prayers, all our good works, all our graces, all our property and possessions, all material and spiritual things, are given to Mary to do with as she wills, to apply as she wills. But Mary's will is one with the will of Jesus. Therefore, we should not fear making the total consecration once we understand it.

Total consecration to Mary is not simply reciting, once in a lifetime, a prayer or formula of consecration. It means living our consecration daily. We should renew the consecration each day, especially when tempted.

(Total consecration to Mary means that we give everything we are and have totally into Mary's hands to do with as she wants.)

174. WHAT IS MEANT BY CATHOLIC LOYALTY TO THE POPE?

Loyalty to the Pope means to obey the Pope as he teaches the faith and morals of the Catholic Church. According to Vatican Council II, not only must we accept the teachings of the Pope when he defines a doctrine of faith or morals, we must accept them at other times as well. That is, the authority of the Pope must be "acknowledged with reverence, the judgments made by him (be) sincerely adhered to, according to his manifest mind and will. His mind and will in the matter may be known chiefly either from the character of the documents, from his frequent repetition of the same doctrine, or from his manner of speaking." Catholics are obligated to obey the Pope in all things pertaining to faith and morals and therefore to the glory of God and the salvation of their immortal souls.

(Catholic loyalty to the Pope means to obey the Pope at all times and to listen to what he has to say because the Pope speaks for Jesus.)

175. DOES DEVOTION TO MARY DEMAND LOYALTY TO OUR HOLY FATHER, THE POPE?

Yes. Mary is the Mother of the Church. Mary is the perfect model of everything the Church is and hopes to become as the Church teaches the role of Mary in our salvation. Jesus Christ Himself set up His Church with St. Peter, the first Pope, as the visible head of His Church after He would ascend into heaven. The Pope today is the visible head of the Church upon earth. Catholics are obliged to obey the laws of the Church, the moral laws of right and wrong, what is true faith, according to the teachings of the Pope. This is the way Jesus Himself founded His Church. Mary as Mother of the Church requires loyalty to the Pope, the visible head, the chief guardian of the faith. As the Woman of Faith, devotion to Mary requires loyalty to the chief guardian of true faith.

(Yes. Mary is the Woman of Faith in the Bible.

*The Bible teaches us that the Pope is the chief guardian
of true faith. Devotion to the Woman of Faith demands
that we listen to and obey the guardian of faith who is
the Pope.)*

176. DOES DEVOTION TO MARY AND CONSE-CRATION TO MARY REQUIRE OBEYING THE TEN COMMANDMENTS?

Yes. The motive for obeying the Ten Commandments of God is love. When one loves God he obeys the Commandments. Devotion to Mary is best expressed in the love of her Immaculate Heart. Mary herself as the perfect member and Mother of the Church was a mother of love. To imitate Mary's love and faith and to love Mary herself requires obeying the Commandments. Disobedience of the Commandments is sinful and that is what wounds the hearts of Jesus and Mary and requires reparation.

*(Yes. When we obey the Commandments we show
our love for God. Devotion to Mary is loving her Immaculate Heart which leads to God's love.)*

SUMMARY:

Consecration to Mary means more than simply reciting a prayer of consecration. It is a Catholic way of life. One who really understands the consecration is conscious of his love of Jesus in union with Mary each day. Totally consecrated to Jesus through Mary, one gives over all that he is and has, his body, soul, property and possessions, even the graces of his soul, the value of his good works, to the love of Mary. One consecrated to Mary gives his will over to the will of Mary to do with as she likes. This requires long prayer and study before such an act of consecration should be made. It is not made and then forgotten. It is of value only when made with understanding and then lived day by day thereafter.

Some people fear consecrating their entire lives to Mary. But when one understands Mary better, that she is the Mother of the Church, the mediatrix of all graces and that she is one with Jesus in everything, such fears disappear. Mary keeps nothing for herself. Mary is inseparable from Jesus. Consecration to Mary is going back to God the way He first came to us in Jesus, that is, through Mary. Jesus still remains the one necessary Mediator (bridge) with God the Father when we consecrate ourselves to Jesus through Mary.

Individuals can consecrate themselves to Mary's Immaculate Heart. Bishops can consecrate their dioceses as the Pope has consecrated the world to Mary. Pastors can consecrate their parishes. Parents can and should consecrate their families to Mary's heart.

QUESTIONS:

1. Why does love for and consecration to Mary not take away from love for Jesus?

2. Is the main thing about consecration to Mary the reciting of a consecration prayer? Explain answer.

3. Why does devotion to Mary require loyalty and obedience to the Pope?

4. Why does devotion to Mary's Immaculate

Heart require obeying the Ten Commandments?

PRACTICE:

If you are not yet prepared for total consecration to Mary forever, offer your life today to Mary's heart and renew it daily until you better understand total consecration.